CU00694111

Collected Poems
1941-1983

MICHAEL HAMBURGER

COLLECTED POEMS
1941-1983

Carcanet Press · Manchester

First published in Great Britain 1984
by the Carcanet Press
208 Corn Exchange Building
Manchester M4 3BQ

This second impression corrects misprints and spacing errors
from the first printing, and supersedes that volume.

The publisher acknowledges financial assistance
from the Arts Council of Great Britain

British Library Cataloguing in Publication Data

Hamburger, Michael
Collected poems.
I. Title
821'.914   PR6015.A414

ISBN 0-85635-497-X

Typesetting by Bryan Williamson, Swinton, Berwickshire
Printed in Great Britain by SRP Ltd., Exeter

Contents

II   The Dual Site 1952-1957

III   Of Time and Place 1957-1964

IV

V   Observations, Ironies, Unpleasantries

VI   Needs and Pastimes 1973-1974

VII   Later Poems

11

VIII   Variations

IX   Dream Poems

For Anne

Author's Note

This collection is entirely due to the generosity and loyalty of my publisher, Michael Schmidt. But for his wish to mark my sixtieth birthday with an omnibus volume I should have had no incentive or inclination to put together what amounts to a complete gathering of my verse to date. If the completeness does not extend to work I wrote and published before 1952, it is because I have long ceased to recognize most of it as mine. That stumbling-block alone might well have deterred me from preparing a *Collected Poems*.

My first impulse, therefore, was to leave out all the early poems or relegate them to an appendix of juvenilia — though I reached the age of twenty-eight in 1952. At that juncture I also favoured a genetic arrangement of the collection as a whole. When I realized that an overall genetic arrangement was beyond me, because my later work, too, did not fall into clear-cut kinds, I decided to confront my early work again, to make a new selection from it, and not to exclude it from a predominantly chronological arrangement.

To prefer an order not based on mere chronological sequence is one thing, quite another to disentangle the threads, or trace the seams and streams, of a progression that now strikes me as having been anything but straightforward. My quarrel with the bulk of the early work is that it tried to leap straight from the personal to the general, not by way of observed phenomena but through archetypes drawn from religion, myth or litera-ture; that it had no stomach at all for the roughage of lived experience. Since that shortcut made me prolific at the time, there could be no question of including all those sonnets, songs, monologues, and ranting jeremiads about the evils of the age; but by selecting from them again, in the context of a *Collected Poems*, I could be less grudging than in earlier selections made for *Penguin Modern Poets* or for *Ownerless Earth*, if the new selection was guided less by impersonal considerations of accomplishment than by personal ones of continuity and completeness. On those grounds I was able to include a number of poems previously rejected even for early books; not because I think them better than the rest, or good enough, but because, however vicariously, they register some of the shocks and conflicts carried over into later work, and as pointers to extreme dualities that had to be bridged or resolved. A few small emendations were called for in the poems added on those grounds. In others I had already excised sententious punch lines I could no longer endure.

Instead of smoother sonnets celebrating poets like Nerval, Baudelaire, Mallarmé and Rimbaud, I have salvaged a rejected one, *November*, that was not second-hand, and hardly got away with being a sonnet at all. I have also included other poems that recall my years of military service in Britain and abroad, formative years to which not only literariness, but often the practical impossibility of writing, prevented me from responding immediately and directly. A condensed version of the previously rejected monologue *Rimbaud in Africa* was chosen in preference to more polished ones on Faustus, Don Juan and Sir Walter Raleigh, not only because in its bookish way it reflects some of the lessons of my military service abroad, but because it prefigures eruptions of anti-poetry that were to recur in later years. For similar reasons I salvaged most of the sequence *From the Notebook of a European Tramp*, even adding a previously rejected part. That this sequence drew on my experiences as a soldier, not a tramp, in post-war Europe, has something to do with its failure to sustain the persona more than sporadically, but its person did have to be a drop-out figure. (At that time I knew a real tramp just as inhibited by his educational and cultural baggage; but that was back in England, and he could be of little use to me as a model in an altogether different setting.)

As for the later work, if completeness and continuity were to be my criteria, it seemed best to record all the by-ways and detours of later journeys, regardless of whether other people or I have come to see them as advances, regressions or dead ends. Such self-criticism as one is capable of is applied at the workshop stage. Though I am aware of fluctuations of intensity, different levels of concentration, among the later poems, and have my own likes and dislikes that would have been operative in a selection, my reasons for rejecting most of the early work do not extend to the later, because I do recognize it as my own.

The overall chronological arrangement has been broken where later poems link on thematically to earlier ones, and over three kinds of poems that strike me as being more or less distinct from the rest. These are the 'Observations, Ironies, Unpleasantries' at one end of my range, the longer sequence I call 'Variations', and the dream poems at the other end. I have also now separated a batch of poems I was asked to write for adolescents, *Needs and Pastimes*, though some of these are close in theme and manner to other verse more didactic than lyrical in the preceding section.

It is not these mild reflective pieces but some of the 'unpleasantries' that have been most disliked by my readers, if not totally ignored. To the objection that they stick out like sore thumbs from the main body of my work, being written in no voice or idiom recognizable as mine, I answer that they are meant to. In the economy of my work they are owls' pellets — gobbets of matter so coarse that it could not be assimilated poetically, only regurgitated. In their way they are persona poems, too, like my early monologues, but persona poems that go to the opposite extreme, a 'low mimetic' of officialese, journalese, salesmanese, or whatever jargon the occasion demanded. That was the only alternative to the satires I could not write, when satire that is also poetry can be written only as long as one is conscious of some sort of general or dominant agreement about public values. In the absence of such consciousness, or such agreement, there was no other way than to borrow the verbiage of those matters, so that the verbiage itself would condemn them.

Some of the most vehement of these 'unpleasantries' are set in America, because in the late sixties and early seventies I spent a good deal of time working there. 'America, love it or leave it!' was a slogan to be read on car stickers and housefronts at the time. If I had not loved a good many people and things in America, as other poems attest, I should not have been moved to write those 'unpleasantries', despite the loves, and despite the hospitality I received in America, before deciding to leave. I include the most drastic of them, *Big Deal* — a piece not previously collected — in the knowledge that it can offend no one whom it does not implicate, and that its irony, in any case, has rebounded on me, now that a great clearance sale of national assets, along Friedmanite lines, has begun in Britain. This unforeseen development does not absolve the author of that piece from the discourtesy of an old world cuckoo, but at least it can no longer be read as an old world sneer. A much later 'unpleasantry', *Recessional*, brings the development home and renders the difficulty, for me, of writing any kind of verse under its shadow.

Apart from early poems not previously collected and a few additions to the later epigrams, partly collected in the pamphlet *Moralities* of 1977, this book includes the uncollected shorter poems I have written since that year. A number of these fell into the sections I have separated from the unclassifiable 'later poems'.

Suffolk, September 1983   M.H.

I

Poems

1941-1951

Hölderlin

(Tübingen, December 1842)

Diotima is dead, and silent
The island's singing bird.
The temple I raised from ruin
Fallen again.

Where is the flame I stoked from ashes
Of the mind? Where are the heroes
And my pulsing song?
Nothing stirs on the lakes of time.
Give back my agony,
O stir the forest's sap,
Sweep my slow blood.

And yet, no caged old panther I,
Pacing my madness. These muttered words
Are gates, not bars, where only I can pass.
This is my wisdom, where no flowers grow,
No weeds, this is my peace.

I am calm now, with the world
Locked out, bowed to the door;
My meadow end is pensioned by the gods.
They did not hear,
O crippled Fate, the grimy idol's
Golden teeth led them away.

I have no tears to mourn forsaken gods
Or my lost voice.
This is my wisdom where no laughter sounds,
No sighs, this is my peace.

Glory is gone, and the swimming clouds;
My dumb hand grips the frozen sky,
A black bare tree in the winter dusk.

From a Train Window

1

A few crumpled leaves
Rattle on widowed branches.
The wind sways these withered rags
Of the dead year.

Over flat fields
Towards a grey horizon
Black wavering flocks of rooks
Wearily flap.

Drowned in the clouds,
Dampened, exhausted, the sun
Wastes its last gilt and ardour,
Tinges the mist.

We stop in a town:
Rows of discoloured houses,
All much alike. Here the mist
Thickens to fog.

2

Now slow flakes fall,
Swan-down, hover,
Cover
With a light pall
Wood, grass and stone.
Gone
Are the shadows and shapes;
Bone-
White, greyish, the street gapes.

November
(Richmond, Yorkshire)

I have watched the hypocritical dawn
And the murderous dusk daubed with lavish hands
On the daily sky, the defeated moon
Slouch away, faintly, where vision ends.

I have walked the ploughed fields and the sharp stubble,
Seeing what was to be seen, the white haze
Draping landscapes of veils around probable
Shapes of level furrows and groping trees,

Till mind would not fill more spaces, remembering
Neither harvest nor noon, nor any summer,
Cloyed with splendour splashed over a mauled world,

Rather (now in the foggy season) yearning
For London, a background of grey, dimmer
Webs of pride by trembling fingers unfurled.

Sentry Duty

His box is like a coffin, but erect.
The night is dull as death. He must not sleep,
But leans against the boards. The night winds creep
Around his face, while the far stars reflect
The awful emptiness of heart and brain,
And trembling wires intone a requiem.
(If they were Sirens he would follow them
Anywhere, anywhere, to their lush domain.)

But no one passes. A stray cat cries out,
The moon emerges from a cloud's dark rim,
And vanishes. He walks, and turns about.

Next day no sad unrest bewilders him
Who'd seen the planets fall into a trance,
The earth shed lustre and significance.

'The Tempest'

An Alternative

I, Prospero, stand on this island's shore,
And from a distance vaguer and more dubious
Than a dream I hear voices as of lovers
Whispering in the night and courtiers jesting.

I recall a tempest that created peace;
But the power that brought forth storms and stillness
Is quite decayed, so they have left me here,
An old man with a bent back, who has outlived
His death.
        Yes, once they called me prince,
(Though then my pride lay elsewhere) until I fled
And made this isle my kingdom, ruling by magic.

I recall a tempest raised for the sake
Of a mortal throne, a night and a day
Of mortal music ... and then this stillness.

Now I bear logs for Caliban whose lust
Has peopled the isle with monsters, begotten
On my daughter; sweet Miranda's grown a hag
With hatching of his slimy progeny.

Perhaps it was a dream (the human voices
And my hoping to follow them) — and a mere dream
Has made me weary — but my master calls, —
I'm coming Caliban. — One night, one day
Lost me my dukedom and my soul's wide realm,
Ariel deserted me and they left me here.

Rimbaud in Africa: A Lost Letter

As tradesmen say everything is worth what it will
fetch, so probably every mental pursuit takes its
reality and worth from the ardour of the pursuer,
being in itself a Nothing.   JOHN KEATS

1

Poems? You would like me to write more poems?
About dusk in the desert, perhaps, dates, camels and thirst?
Mirages?
        Why not, if you pay me well.

So they're talking of me in the salons.
I know the sequence: the salons after the littérateurs,
And lastly the dons.
Verlaine has written about me, called me a poète maudit?
Do they have to put even the curse on paper,
Isn't even the curse my own?

You ask me to think of glory:
An adolescent's dream. I am growing up.
Yes, I hear old Paul has been taught
To sigh most endearingly:
Ladies are weeping over 'Sagesse'.
I leave the glory to him.

So they're talking of me in the salons.
Let them talk! Their words cannot reach me now.
I've travelled far to earn an honest living.

2

Any strumming will do, if it titillates.
There's your glory for which a poet pawns his soul
And vivisects himself —
A topic for the bored, a thesis for the dons.
For that we torment ourselves,
Practise exquisite contortions, melodious anguish.
The birds make happier music.

25

Often at evening a fair pervades
A village with music of roundabouts.
Yet windows are not shut,
And old men's faces melt
With memories. The tunes are flat,
Neat and mechanic as the lives they led.
But if a poet were to raise his voice
Above the noise of traffic
And for a moment silence
Laughter and bargaining and scolding,
The cries of little children would not cease,
Nor a cow raise her head from the grass.
Only, in the asylum garden
One inmate would stop his ears,
And another smile.

3

I was clever when I was young —
Good at Latin, better at blasphemy.
I built myself a hell and furnished it,
Disdained the comfort of other people's heaven.
My hysteria was cosmogenetic, but did not change
One grain of sand in the real world.
A little experience has made me dull.

I have travelled far,
But all my journeys are like the scenes of a play,
Shifting but half-real only;
For I know the players, who are
Always the same, everywhere,
And I know something of the playwright too.

London, Cairo, Paris, Addis-Abbaba
Or villages of the Ardennes:
This earth was made for tourists.
But ask a soldier how he liked the pyramids,
And he'll say that beer is bad in Egypt
And expensive too,
While in Turkey vodka is cheap,

Though the girls are plain.
The Sphinx, at best, makes him regret
The Arc de Triomphe or the Nelson Column.
My journeys are like a soldier's,
Passionless.

Tell my friends in Paris, therefore,
That Rimbaud is dead and likes it,
That even if he were to return
They would not know him, nor he them.
If they speak of a boy
Who wrote verses and thought the angels dumb,
Tell them that thirst is never comic
And that the drunken boat is sober now,
Leaking and battered, only just afloat.
Tell them I do not care
Whether they praise or damn it when it sinks.

A Billet and the Destination
Ulverston, Lancashire

The garden was out of bounds; but jasmine,
Drooping wistaria, rhododendron
Flowered nonetheless in June and cast
Bright petals down.

They scarcely noticed, for their spring was lost
Or hoped for, never present. Summer passed,
And autumn, and when winter came one dark-
Red rose was left.

They were in transit, all their cares and loves
Removed, unreal, their pleasures hazardous.
Not one looked back or spoke a word when, drafted,
They left the house.

They packed and went, seemed not to wonder, where;
And when the soft wind stirred they were far off,
In a hot country, sprawling crooked there,
Dead in wet mud.

Reminiscences of a Voyage

For John Symonds

1

With masts of fever I sailed
Through Biscay purple and Sorrento blue
Towards pale meadows of the Adriatic
Beneath a constant sky.
No seagull shattered the horizon
Or broke the silence, and no gale.

"Can we not set the sapphires of the sea
And take them home?", I asked.
In Capri vineyards a peasant laughed:
    "Yes, photographs we sell,
    Postcards dirty and clean,
    A silver bell
    From San Michel',
    Priapus of Pompeii;
    Coral and mother-of-pearl.
    But sapphires of the sea?"
And we sailed on till the sea was grey.

2

A septic climate. Cynically the sun
Smiles on its festering brood of flesh and fruit.
"O Mother of Love, Venus, Maria,"
A beggar prayed, "we shall soon be dying
Despite the palaces and shrines of saints.
Send us tourists and bread for our children
And wine to drink in your honour. Hear us!

We have sold our girls to the troops, and yet
We go hungry in the streets stripped by war."

On stones of fever I walked and wondered
What city this could be where palm and pine
Were joined, palace and slum; but when the bat
Swooped in the swallow's place and love-sick song
Mixed with the crack of whips, I knew its name.

3

Cities and seas, aspects of the moon
Our parasite, and decrees of the sun,
Patterns of cloud, climates, features of men,
Fishes and insects, houses, flowering trees,
Mountains pine-softened, mountains of stark stone,
Grottoes, lagoons, mere gestures — all these,
And much besides, we saw, took in, compared
And now should like to recollect, had they not faded
Away in mind's grey morning, the voyage past.
Nothing is left of Venice but the sound
Of endless water lapping the dull mind.

From the Notebook of a European Tramp

I

Even in mid-October there is spring
When after frost from Iceland breezes come
All laden with the basking South to bring
Bright life to yellow leaves and warm the numb
Fingers of tramps on sun-forsaken roads;
When the high tide of summer zest rolls back
Out of the veins, and no swift impulse goads
Me onward, onward to a wilder track;
When almost cities like some painted girl
Hold me with sweetly, sickly smelling charms,
So that, half cosmopolitan, half churl,

I flirt in passing with a street's white arms —
Then the warm winds refuel me. I spit
Into the gutter and walk on, a friar
Without a mission, horse without a bit,
Bound for the perfect nowhere of desire.

II

But sometimes the dusk seems boundless; and always
The mountains lie ahead, keeping something
From me, in themselves a secret and guarding
Others in the unattainable plains.
So too the fates of strangers, the fast-rooted
And those uprooted from their sliding worlds,
Move me as they pass by, their faces concrete
But for the eyes, untended pits of fear.
But there's no help for all the landscapes severed
And lost in Europe, or their gaping eyes,
Nor will I pour my glassful of hot pity
Into the ocean that will numb us all.
For none's the hunter now, though all are hunted —
The clinging, the sheltering, the fleeing —
Even I who, walking in the cruel grey
Of the dusk, made uncertainty my home.

III

"Christmas will break your heart," an old hand said,
"Such stillness and the churchbells crying out,
And you alone in the cold; —you'll not be glad
You chose to be a lousy gadabout."
It's Christmas now and all is just the same;
The snow's no deeper than it was last week,
The night's no quieter; why should a name
Melt the old fellow's guts and make him meek?
Surely a wretched scribbler gone astray!
To hoard up Christian love the whole year round
And pour it all into a single day,
Stale sickly seed into exhausted ground!
In the tramp's calendar Christmas is when

30

He's one with all things, squirrel, toad and sow,
Even the richest of his fellow men,
That is, at any time and anyhow.
As for my heart, it broke some time ago
When, in the towns of Europe, I still tried
To live like other men and not to know
That all we lived for had already died.

IV

Sun and snow; yet in my head
Town thoughts, street griefs revolve,
Problems which I did not solve
When I was tame and led
A domesticated life,
Read the papers and could
Not guess that ever I should
Eat with a pocket-knife.

Mid-February; but here
Winter drips from the trees;
Higher up small boys on skis,
Virtuosi of fear,
Embody the unborn spring
That gives them mastery.
Surely my mind should not be
Bothered with anything.

Moon and snow; I am the same
Poor fool who maunders down
Every street of every town
And does not need a name,
Since the arc-lights cast a sheen
Not clear enough to trace
Much more than a basic face,
Eyes that seek the unseen.

In the distance dogs bark; perhaps high up
On the mountain-sides, where peasants have built
Those desolate houses that shine like stars
At night, and in the day-time seem hardly real.
Yet there they live all winter, immune to awe
Of the blue night, closed to the silence, blind
To the passing of apocalyptic clouds.
And in spring-time too they endure, unstirred
By the melting transalpine breezes, the fall
Of icicles from the eaves, the fleeing streams.

But I, a hardened tramp, walk on below,
Gaping at beauty and even now not sure
What it is I have gone to find, seeking
A freedom that's mine already, or no one's.
And like a tourist whose guide-book is lost,
Whose wonderment is a wound, an emptiness,
Sometimes I wish I were safely caged at home,
Sheltered from the caprices of the year,
The moods of the moon, less clumsily in love
With the cosmetic surface of the earth.

VI

Still in Vienna longing upholsters
The past, old bones are wrapped up in our rags;
Too late. These palaces are forever dead;
Though the facades are patched, voluptuous
Foliage of stucco restored to the porches,
Gold splashed lavishly over lustres and walls,
Never shall breath or sound stir them again.
What should the mirrors reflect? the hungry
Faces of tourists thrust in and withdrawn
Or the officials so clumsily caged
In paper glory dry as the beams beneath,
Their narrow power like collars, starched, stifling them? —
And though its twisted saints seem nearer to us,
Tuned to our pitch of pain, St Stephen's rises

Slender and straight to a different heaven.
No sudden blast lifted its roof; but long
Before the bombs the buttresses relaxed.
A rounder pomp, the too inflated cherubs came,
Unhoused the Gothic God and died of gout;
Both now are stone forever, motionless.

VII

That the creative mind might rest and trees
Might flatter it like household grenadiers,
The pride of kings besieged by mortal fears
Planned gardens as impeccable as these;
Caserta, Schoenbrunn, Sanssouci, Versailles:
The water canalized, strict symmetry
Of column, statue, path, periphery,
Bounded but boundless to the scanning eye.

Till truant flowers and weeds like dancing fauns
Broke through that sterile stillness and cried out;
Soon sandwich wrappings blossomed on the lawns.
The tortured tourist came and lounged about;
But from that Eden built for Adams dead,
Eves obsolete, even the dream had fled.

VIII

Displaced Persons' Camp

Is it because the pursuing past is named,
The desired future, the refuge dreamed of
Is indexed, that here among the lost there is
A little hope, while outside there is none?
These, the outwardly displaced who live in huts,
Who fled with nothing but a rug, ikon
Or song salvaged and their native languages,
Cheerfully queue for their daily soup, gossip
And, child-like, take delight in accidents,
Sucking calamity like stolen sweets.

In the evenings the smugglers barter goods,
From hut to hut, from room to room: grappa
And thread from Italy, old boots, tinned meat,
Coffee, gold coins, tobacco, opium,
All the conflicting poisons and necessities.
But when the Kolo unwinds at night and their feet
Obey old rhythms, when older song, carefree
Or melting slowly to the concertina's sadness,
Grips them entirely, time ceases and they are
As much at home as they have ever been.

IX

The townsman on his yielding bed
Thinks that the world will end when he
Sleeps on the wooden boards instead.
He also who was forced to see
The mind's own mattresses ripped up
And many a recipient head
Smashed like a saucer or a cup
Feels that by rights he should be dead.

At times perhaps he even finds
That metaphysics were no more
Than luxury of idle minds,
And he a simpleton before —
Particularly in the spring
When chaos, as of old, unbinds
Gods who are game for anything
And demigods of various kinds.

In winter he is not so sure
And says his prayers just in case
A word in the right place might cure
His ailments, save him from disgrace.
And still it seems a little weird
That the earth's axle is secure
When all the nightmares he most feared
Prosper in sunlight and endure.

X

Their hands are cranes descending that can only grasp
Substances massed and named. They clutch, lift up, swing
    round,
Lower, release their loads. Relax? The engine throbs,
And only late at night the winding wheels are still,
The metal muscles loose, the empty fist unclenched.

Their feet are hammers that stamp down the living grass,
Crush all the wildflowers and choke the lesser springs.
Beetles and butterflies lie crumpled in their tracks,
And husks of hours in which undying seed had lain
Blow endlessly along the gutters of dead years.

Oh, if their hands could linger, loving what they touch,
And if their feet could feel the living carpet's texture,
Time, that both fuels and consumes them now, would end;
And where the sweeping net, though swift and furious, failed,
Slow fingers gather more than they have dared to seek.

XI

Berlin, 1947

They too were told the facts, they too were taught
An alphabet of bliss and all the rules.
But the same shop in which their wealth was bought
Buys nothing back; the shop-girl ridicules
The candlesticks and pictures they have brought,
And all the glory learnt by heart in schools
Is worthless junk and bric-à-brac that ought
To have been burnt or buried by the fools.

Cheated, they turn away. Some search the street
For fag-ends dropped by God and never found,
Till rage accelerates their scraping feet,
Patience peels off like summer skin, the ground,
Hearts, houses, heaven are spinning giddily
And knowledge licks them like the waiting sea.

XII

Eyes cruel with abjection glare
In trams packed full, and bleached lips grin
At the limp silence which despair
Assumes in what was once Berlin.
Eyes naked in their hunger stare
At each new body squeezing in,
Assess its wealth in calories,
Guess how much longer it might last.
Death has its inequalities,
Creates distinctions, rank and caste:
All may be dying by degress,
But some die slowly, some die fast.

XIII

"When the bombs have done their worst, when the winds
Play with the water, forgetting Venice
And London is a healing wound in the plains,
When the dust has settled where Paris stood,
Perhaps the golden age will return, all men
At last be brothers and tramps, the earth
Belong to all, brain and muscle count again."
But we have sold our tricks to South and East,
Rifles and cant, the mechanical itch,
The Congo ticks with our clocks and China
Is torn by slogans;
                    therefore be patient,
Keep your books or others will teach you to read
And where Eden should be new towns will rise.
I know that you are weary and waiting
For the ultimate spring, the purging
Touch of breezes, the sun on your backs,
But a little civilization is worse
Than too much; so don't let old Europe die
Nor think your sons and daughters will be free
To bask like lizards on discarded stone.
Live a little, be patient, mock or rebuild,
Admire, before the bombs have done their worst.

XIV

It is not war that matters now — until
In the last city the last lamp sickens,
Nothing is lost; but whether soon that night
Against which all our lamps and fires were lit
Will draw us back, so that the dappled fields,
Oceans and pulsing woods are desolate,
Our eyes are maggots lusting after death.
Stone and more stone is heaped about our heads,
Till bombs may turn to thunderbolts, God's gift
To children whose last toy has been explored.

XV

A windless April; blossom white and still
Suspended on the twigs, immobilized.
Soft, silent night heavy with muted thunder,
A terrible sweetness, life itself embalmed.
Ghostly, the lightning plays on a velvet sky.
Time too is running down: it is the end.
Creep quietly to sleep, you that are left;
Do not complain. You too have never been
More than the mirrors of a dying world,
Though once you thought that spring melts into summer,
The soil that nourished could receive your flesh
And sucking roots convey you to the leaves.
But now the soil is dead; lie down and sleep.
You slept no better in your linen sheets,
Nor I on benches, boards and borrowed beds.
Perhaps of all the landscapes we have seen,
Waking or sleeping, one can still deceive
The bare horizon of our final dream.

XVI

Wherever I may die
Dig in what's left and let it lie;
I never cared for fame,
The brief survival of a name.

37

These pages too you may
Leave where they'll share in my decay
Or you make take them out
And let the wind blow them about.
Though books and gravestones are
Sublime while perpendicular,
They'll tumble, as prostrate
As that which they commemorate,
And I would rather pass
Into the nameless green of grass,
Where still, alive or dead,
Tramp-like, I shall not rise but spread.

Grodek: In Memorian Georg Trakl

"In the evening the autumn woods cry out
With deadly weapons and the golden plains,
The deep blue lakes, above which more darkly
Rolls the sun; the night embraces
Dying warriors, the wild lament
Of their broken mouths."
But the wounds of others are lightly borne,
There is an end to war, sooner or later
The living will be counted and sent home.
"Every street leads to blackest carrion.
Under golden twigs of the night and stars ..."
Surely he could outlive this night; harden
Against the morning, blind himself
As the others did and refuse to feel?
But his was a different courage:
To see and to bleed with seeing,
The skin of his senses unbandaged, his brain unfenced.
When his nerve broke, they locked him up.
"And softly the dark flutes of autumn sound
In the reeds." The wounds of others
Would never heal, he would drag for ever
On others' crutches; he died of pity.
Cursing, they dug him in.

T.S. Eliot

A Tribute

I

Almost it was too late, near closing-time
For Europe when he came to gather up
Whatever petals wind and broom had spared
In the last garden; there it was he heard
The laughter of belated children leap
Before the outraged keeper sent them home.

Then it was night; a sprawling town stretched out
Sick limbs where temporary lovers walked,
While in the distance dying trumpeters
Blared insult and self-pity at the stars.
He studied patience; and when next he looked
Some kind of dawn quivered on dirty slate.

II

But in the heart's Antarctic, between sound
And silence, where the boundary of dreams
Meets memory, pausing, at last he found
Music and mastery for winter themes.

Garden and streets were gone, though twilight kept
Both vaguely visible, the frozen air
Recalled how once the children's mirth had leapt,
And how the trumpeters had known despair.

To a Deaf Poet

Silence is our harbour but remembered seas
Provide our wealth; how then, when often we
With all our ships and nets know poverty,
Is it that you bound to an island sit
So patiently on the dry shore of music,
Not waiting only but slowly gathering

Shells we, the hurrying, had overlooked?
Your feeling fingers hear
Vibrations of the sea in solid things,
The pebbles weighted with lost whisperings,
Or, drained of sound but mutely echoing,
The washed-up revelations of the drowned.

Flowering Cactus

In Memoriam Jankel Adler

Worlds too can be transplanted, alien griefs cry out,
A foreign ecstasy explode in our own house
Or suddenly a desert on the window-sill
Burst into purest red. Great metamorphosis
Which from a shrivelled cactus conjures liquid fire,
Answering absent solitudes and wastes of sky!
Worlds too can wilt; the same green body in whose veins
Visions were stored, sand, water, light were taught to speak
Is parched beyond endurance: yellow now, then brown,
Its flesh hints at no knowledge of potential flowers.

The Death of an Old Man

Muttering at the crowd, indifferent
Faces which could not understand that he,
An island full of wilting flowers pent
In by the foolish, the forgetting sea,
Was rare and beautiful, quite suddenly
He plunged into the traffic, his neck bent
Low like a fighting bull's who seems intent
On the quick blade but, bleeding, cannot see.

Then he awoke, his body broken, knew
What had happened. In the dusk his mind
Began its last descent, let pain review
The landscape he could neither leave behind

Nor take away; for who will now unwind
His memory, relive past love, renew
The music and the silences that grew
Within him for a life-time, intertwined?

London Tomcat

Look at the gentle savage, monstrous gentleman
With jungles in his heart, yet metropolitan
As we shall never be; who — while his human hosts,
Afraid of their own past and its primaeval ghosts,
Pile up great walls for comfort — walks coquettishly
Through their elaborate cares, sure of himself and free
To be like them, domesticated, or aloof!
A dandy in the room, a demon on the roof,
He's delicately tough, endearingly reserved,
Adaptable, fastidious, rope-and-fibre-nerved.
Now an accomplished Yogi good at sitting still,
He ponders ancient mysteries on the window-sill,
Now stretches, bares his claws and saunters off to find
The thrills of love and hunting, cunningly combined.
Acrobat, diplomat, and simple tabby cat,
He conjures tangled forests in a furnished flat.

Paddington Canal

A mocking mirror, the black water turns
Tall houses upside down, makes learned men
Walk on their heads in squares of burning light;
Lovers like folded bats hang in a kiss,
Swaying as if a breeze could sever them.
The barges, giant sea-birds fast asleep,
Lie on the surface, moored and motionless;
Then, drowning gently, are drawn down to join
The sunken lovers and the acrobats.

41

Out of the grim dimensions of a street
Slowly I see another landscape grow
Downwards into a lost reality;
A magic mirror, the black water tells
Of a reversed Atlantis wisely built
To catch and to transform
The wasted substance of our daily acts,
Accommodate our mad and lovely doubles
In a more graceful city timelessly.

A Legend

I

Simone del Manzecca di Poggio

What, on that hill, was there to do but love?
Dark woods were round about: cypress and oak,
While olives near that other castle spoke
In whispers he had never heard above.

And there was prayer; but the pagan sun,
Birdsong and bells, roses and yellow broom,
The Tuscan vineyards and his own white room,
The gazing sky fed every sense but one.

What could he pray for, when his loneliness
Was rich as any painted Paradise,
But that, before it killed him, he might know
Rest from this beauty's terrible excess,
Which — so his longing told him — would suffice
To drown another in its overflow?

II

Below the battlements, Selvaggia waited;
Simone and her father had come back
Together from the war. Now the steep track
She stared at should be safe. She hesitated:

For from Maiano, towards Fiesole,
A swollen moon rose overripe and red;
It seemed to her that its intrusion shed
Spilt gold or blood on every olive-tree.

Gold of the unobtainable, his blood.
She saw them kill him, saw the landscape turn
A somersault, and heard how both towers fell;
The moon, his helmet, sizzled in the mud.
Thinking that before long the earth would burn,
She ran till madness cooled her like a well.

A Poet's Progress

Like snooker balls thrown on the table's faded green,
Rare ivory and weighted with his best ambitions,
At first his words are launched: not certain what they mean,
He loves to see them roll, rebound, assume positions
Which—since not he—some power beyond him has assigned.
But now the game begins: dead players, living critics
Are watching him — and suddenly one eye goes blind,
The hand that holds the cue shakes like a paralytic's,
Till every thudding, every clinking sound portends
New failure, new defeat. Amazed, he finds that still
It is not he who guides his missiles to their ends
But an unkind geometry that mocks his will.

If he persists, for years he'll practise patiently,
Lock all the doors, learn all the tricks, keep noises out,
Though he may pick a ghost or two for company
Or pierce the room's inhuman silence with a shout.
More often silence wins; then soon the green felt seems
An evil playground, lawless, lost to time, forsaken,
And he a fool caught in the water weeds of dreams
Whom only death or frantic effort can awaken.

At last, a master player, he can face applause,
Looks for a fit opponent, former friends, emerges;
But no one knows him now. He questions his own cause,
And has forgotten why he yielded to those urges,
Took up a wooden cue to strike a coloured ball.
Wise now, he goes on playing; both his house and heart
Unguarded solitudes, hospitable to all
Who can endure the cold intensity of art.

Judas Iscariot

No part was harder than his and none more cruel:
To be God's chosen villain in the absolute play,
Cast out by friends and enemies, cast out of self,
Hated by all for ever, hating himself;
And that the sinuous prophecy might be fulfilled,
Wriggle, a viper, down the appointed path,
Dust on his tongue,
Till he was dry and twisted as the final rope.

Pilate could speak of duty, Peter of human fear
Keener than love; but Judas could not speak,
For he had ripped out fear with the roots of love
And his inhuman duty was unspeakable.
Dust in his heart,
The inmost source of language clogged with dust,
He dreamed of sleep,
How in the end one drowsy snake would meet another,
Coiled in a dumb, yet passionate embrace.

44

That was the second kiss;
The first — how long ago it seemed — had killed him.
Might not the second give him life again?
Myopic men would hate him — so the play demanded —
But would the Master who gazed with different eyes?
A maze, a mystery was justice; only this he knew:
In God's own forge he had been melted down,
By God's own hammer beaten into murderous shape,
Betrayed into betraying.
After the deed, might not the instrument rest?

Or could it be that when the curtain fell on the last scene,
When, silent, the spectators stumbled home,
Still the actors were not dismissed, but in the dark
Must re-enact their parts?
If it was true that shroud and sepulchre could not contain
The Master's fiery spirit,
Then he for ever too, as Christ was Christ,
For ever must be Judas
And in a hell of cold self-hatred bite his tail.

Sleep, then, would be no refuge: never would he shed
His dark imprisoning skin, the dust of that long day,
Nor ever in the sweet still water bathe.

Islands

Cold winds cannot freeze
Nor the frozen centuries
Weigh on these lovers who walk
Under April's blossoming trees,
Whitethorn, apple and pear.
Though the river drown the fields
And, crying out, the hours
Crash from the cruel towers,
They'll walk in the waking year.

Reflecting on love's one law,
In the flooded fields I saw
A nesting swan at rest.
Magpie, rook, jackdaw
Hovered cawing above
Their pasture lost in the tide
Where the mated swans had found
An isolated mound
For their long and island love.

Islands only remain:
An island of light in the lane
And these lingering lovers lapped
In the darkened city's disdain.
Another island glows
In the glassy fields beyond
Where veiled in vapours of night,
Slender and opal-white,
Two sleeping swans repose.

In October

In October a pregnant woman walked by the river
When autumn's failing green on the water's face
Conjures a world without depth, a landscape of glass.
She saw leaves and their images meet and saw them severed,
From the tall trees, glowing, a flicker of red fall down,
Leaves of the weeping willow drop and drown,
Cracking that mirror of green, the immaculate water.
"Tears of time", she thought, "O my son or daughter
Due to be born with the lambs and, like them, slaughtered,
By the sudden thrust in war, slow waste in peace,
To wonder, to hope for a while, then glimmer passionless.
Man's grief I perpetuate, which else would cease."

Faint, but golden, the sun broke through the haze.
She saw dead leaves assembled on the river's bed,
Water weeds groping for food, their green unshed,
And, above, new buds, minute, on the naked boughs.
"Nameless you are", she thought, "my son or daughter,
Nameless as unborn leaves, dead leaves and the water,
A particle, passing, but blessed, between never and always.
Man's joy I perpetuate, the tree and the river,
Summer's unbroken mirror, the cracking glass
And the stillness that spreads where leaf and image divide."

A Brief Biography

This poor amphibian on the dry land of prose
Watched others labour; now hoped to emulate
The troubled ant who, gathering details, goes
Patiently about his business, to create;
Now sickened by the sight, he envied fish —
Whose yielding element, it seemed, fulfilled
Their faintest, mute unformulated wish
Lest impulse should grow weak by being willed —
For foolishly, deliciously intent
On self-expression, all day long they played
In the clear liquid of abandonment,
Poetic palaces of light and shade ...
Then with the ducks became identified,
Domestic, democratic, sociable,
Not over-clean, but innocent of pride,
Products of humble homesteads and the Fall ...
Till he saw swans — a pair of them — and knew:
Art is aristocratic. Lend me pure white
To glide on time's calm waters or in the blue
Expanse of summer answer the infinite!

Oh, he was none of these; could scarcely swim,
Not walk at all, nor fly, nor work, nor play.
What most he loved most cruelly wounded him
By being loveliest when he turned away.

47

He could sit still for hours, catch a few flies —
A modest minimum — on his floating log,
But soon would languish for the great surprise,
Proof that he was not what he was, a frog.

Ants climbed and stumbled, fell and climbed once more,
The leisured fishes glittered in glassy streams,
Ducks paddled, dived or waddled on the shore,
The swans, two distant lovers, guarded their dreams.
He gazed and hoped and envied, rarely tried,
Yet, always changing, giddily revolved,
Restless till in the unremembering tide
His tortured multiplicity dissolved.

Lines on Brueghel's 'Icarus'

The ploughman ploughs, the fisherman dreams of fish;
Aloft, the sailor through a world of ropes
Guides tangled meditations, feverish
With memories of girls forsaken, hopes
Of brief reunions, new discoveries,
Past rum consumed, rum promised, rum potential.
Sheep crop the grass, lift up their heads and gaze
Into a sheepish present: the essential,
Illimitable juiciness of things,
Greens, yellows, browns are what they see.
Churlish and slow, the shepherd, hearing wings —
Perhaps an eagle's — gapes uncertainly;

Too late. The worst had happened: lost to man,
The angel, Icarus, for ever failed,
Fallen with melted wings when, near the sun
He scorned the ordering planet, which prevailed
And jeering, now slinks off, to rise once more.
But he — his damaged purpose drags him down —
Too far from his half-brothers on the shore,
Hardly conceivable, is left to drown.

The Reconciliation

Their grief, though separate, was the same,
Bound each to the other, like a child;
Till — pride had wearied of the game —
Stranger to stranger was reconciled.

Reversal

From their source how easily
Dark artesian sorrows rise
And more like pleasures play
Transfused with daylight in her eyes.

Ah, but I told her so:
Now reversed those fountains race
From her dry but sullen face,
Daylight even sucked below.

II

The Dual Site

1952-1957

Palinode

A daily vision broke my rage:
The beauty of a cold white page,
Bare island in a polar sea
Whose terrible virginity
A hymen of deep ice defends.
Here the familiar voyage ends;
But, though becalmed, at last I know
The heat that radiates from snow.
     Flies on the window-pane,
     My words have buzzed in vain.

Or southern landscapes: child and nun
Turned into objects by the sun;
All emptied by a light so strong
That on the hill the ploughman's song
Was no less natural than the breeze
Which bore it through the olive-trees.
Harsh as blue grapes, his voice conveyed
Dark due to sunshine, not to shade.
     An animal's ecstasy or pain,
     Ambiguous, echoed through the plain.

And there a bullfight purged the heart
Of comforts fiction adds to art,
Applying Aristotle's law,
Pity and terror, in the raw:
This hero's flesh confirmed the plot.
No, never Jove, nor Juggernaut
Smiled on the trembling jade that bore
Pain's padded priest, the picador.
     Where gushing blood is plain
     Will sand absorb the stain?

Recant, recant the tenderness
That flows too easily. Confess:
Well shod against the jagged stalk
We tender-footed poets walk

On horrors multiple as grass,
A luscious carpet—pause, but pass;
And like the matador's, our skill
Is wasted if we cannot kill.
> Loud in the weather-vane
> Unfeeling winds complain.

Kill every creature, beast and bird,
Flower and ourselves, to feed the Word,
Our last Chimaera never found
Till we have covered desert ground
With serpents, goats, and lions killed
For the one site on which to build
An egocentric heap of stones
Inscribed: Bellerophon — his bones.
> Yet not for so much gain:
> Vanished summits we attain.

To climb and voyage in the heat
Prepared me for a worse defeat:
This last and loveliest anchorage
Where a cold summer broke my rage.
Explorers dying here, on seas
Rigid with Time's own cruelties,
Gasped out another vision too:
A town ... white marble ... veined with blue.
> Lost is the song in the plain;
> Raked in the blood-red stain;
> Silent the weather-vane.

The Sacrifice

"We are not deathless but you make us so,
Being the dreadful Emperor for whose sake
We are about to die and dying seek
None but a posthumous honour, your applause,
No boon but this you've granted us, a cause:
Your dubious distance from the men we know."

Distant indeed, that Emperor is gone,
And long before his fall had ceased to note
Whose was the point and whose the punctured throat,
Bored past endurance with their martyrdom.
The plebs alone gave every face a name,
Counting the wounds he would not look upon.

Now some went wild because afraid to doubt,
So wild, they could not wait until the day,
But mauled their guards and died without delay.
Others, unfit for arms, were loosed in packs
To pitch their bulk at undefended backs
Though whores and hangmen hissed the knockabout.

The best betrayed suspicion in a twist
Lent to the formal greeting, showed the skill
Of nonchalant courage, but grew loath to kill.
The cause held good: present or absent, he —
More than himself — must bless their agony;
And, bad at murder, here they'd not be missed.

The Emperor's usurper, too, is dead.
But even now, they say, from time to time
A good man wins and, punished for that crime
In contravention of the ancient laws,
Hears ghostly words grow faint, the god's applause,
Dying in doubt, yet strangely comforted.

Respite

In the almost birdless wood
Unstirring long I stood.
A buzzard hovered above;
I listened — but he alone
As if in torment cried
Over the littered stone,
Table and altar, where dove,
Young magpie and rabbit had died
To still the doom in his blood.

Now silken fur and feather,
White-flaked with dung, together
Glow in the gold-streaked gloom,
An iridescence shed
On the living darkness of moss:
As jewels, radiantly dead,
Glint in an open tomb
These relics cast their gloss
On bracken, stone and heather.

Silence has blotted pain
In the Savage God's domain.
The buzzard, looping, has glided
High over moor and hill;
Yet folded in faint unease
For a moment all is still
Where his wind-blurred cry subsided,
A deathly diocese
Waiting to praise and complain.

The Dual Site

To my twin who lives in a cruel country
    I wrote a letter at last;
For my bones creaked out in our long silence
    That seven years had passed,

Seven whole years since he and I
    By word or token exchanged
The message I dare not do without:
    That still we are not estranged,

Though I watch figures in a city office
    And he the waves of the sea,
Keeping no count since he hardly cares
    What happens to him or to me;

Since to names and numbers he closed his head
   When, children still, we were parted,
Chose birth and death for his calendar,
   But leaves the dates uncharted,

Being one who forgets what I remember,
   Who knows what I do not,
Who has learnt the ways of otter and raven
   While I've grown polyglot.

Lately I found a cactus in flower
   And feared for his apple-trees,
Dozed in the club and saw his cattle
   Drag with a foul disease,

And my bones grown stiff with leaning and lying
   Cried out that I'll labour in vain
Till I help my twin to rebuild his hovel
   That's open to wind and rain.

So I sent him a note, expecting no answer,
   And a cheque he'd never cash,
For I knew he was one who'd smile if he heard
   His own roof come down with a crash,

But above the porpoise-leaping bay
   Where ploughshare fin and tail
Cut furrows the foam-flecked sea fills up
   He'd stand in the swishing gale,

Calm as the jackdaws that nest in crannies
   And no more prone to doubt,
With gull and cormorant perched on the rocks
   Would wait the weather out.

Yet he wrote by return: "Have no fear for your dwelling
   Though dry-rot gnaws at the floors;
Only lighten their load of marble and metal,
   Keep clear the corridors,

Move out the clocks that clutter your study,
    And the years will leave you alone:
Every frame I know of lasts long enough,
    Though but cardboard, wood or bone.

And spare me your nightmares, brother, I beg you,
    They make my daemons laugh,
They scare the spirits that rarely will visit
    A man with no wand or staff,

With no symbol, no book and no formula,
    No lore to aid him at all,
Who wherever he walks must find the image
    That holds his mentors in thrall.

But your waking cares put down on paper
    For me to give to the wind,
That the seed may fall and the dry leaf crumble,
    Not a wisp he left behind

Of the tangle that hides the dual site
    Where even you and I
Still may meet again and together build
    One house before we die."

Season and Circumstance

Sentence and Reply

I

Prison of circumstance, a foolproof sky,
Till death deliver him, shall bound his day
Who, blessed with folly, sheltered prudently,

Forsook his joy, to feel the rivers flow,
Put sheep to graze in meadows lush and low,
Lazed on the banks and watched his flock decay

With fat and foot-rot. Leave him to regret
The bordering hills might save them from their plight
Or else in sudden transit decimate

His weight of wealth who loved to travel light —
Living by skill in losing his estate —
Scorned name, relation, number ... and would yet,

Could he but move. Make wind and waterfall,
Wingbeat of birds returning, cuckoo's call,
Ever more distant, taunt his dwindled will

And though with melted snow the river swell,
Flooding his land, let it be winter still
For him alone who once was mutable

But fearing death, turned traitor to the dead,
Bargained for time and shirked his proper trade,
Catastrophe, which now discomfited,

He longs to brave but cannot, his choice made.

II

Love led me always. Love detains me now.
A one-way course, one river I follow,
Rushed with it shallow, deeper go slow.

The water feeds which brushed the rooted willow
To lay bare wood for the slow rain to kill
And with its rot replace eroded soil.

Restless in spring we travel, sooner to be still,
Dare out of fear what most we fear to know
And only plunge because afraid to fall;

More surely balanced, seem equivocal,
Past fear of falling, have no wish to climb,
Adept at nearly drowning, tempt no squall.

The sentence I approve, deny the crime:
Who serves a single season serves them all,
Serving the seasons never can serve time.

A pool I choose. It robs no waterfall,
Meshed with lush weeds would stop no rapid's flow.
I've crossed the hills that prove my pastures low

And here shall stay, unenvious of the swallow
Since moved or wintering always I have my will.
Spring wind and flood show best what stalks are hollow:

I'll cut no reeds and let the creepers grow.

Philoctetes

The sky grows dumb, the seasons of my pain
Are not the mainland seasons.
Contracted in this wound my thought grows blind
And I blaspheme
Because the island of my wound is loud.
Now that I doubt this bow's divinity
I am the beasts I feed on, less than the birds
That only visit here, though here they fall
Pierced by my hated arrows.

Once I could picture archipelagos,
Prayed to the binding sea
To grant me news of those I left behind,
News of my father and of Heracles,
The living and the dead.
The sea grows dumb and I grow separate
Confined to Lemnos where the tide is pain,
A festering foot the seasons —
Now that I doubt this wound's divinity.

Once I could search the clouds for images,
Could strain my ears for some redeeming voice
Vouchsafed by Heracles —
The sun's blind eye moved in a labyrinth
And sparks of no great fire the stars went out.
No message, but the stillness of despair,
Dumb rocks, the deafened sea,
And every cry my separate agony,
Cacophonous echo in my stinking lair.

Wrong after wrong, the prowling cats of the sea:
Tricked by a mortal, here ends prophecy:
If by Odysseus' cunning Troy is taken
In godless peace Hellas will waste away —
Now numb, now sore — their fate
To live on Lemnos, long for Thessaly
Till in the glutinous air
No bird can break their seasons and no prayer
Travel towards the mainland of their pain.

Survivor's Song

Tumble and break, my brittle words,
Bricks from a building the blast has hit.
A fine house it was; and I lived in it.
Long ago. In all that street
Nothing now is the same,
Only the site and the name.

As once with boulders on the beach,
With rubble I played a lonely game
Or listened to the silly birds
Who chirping, trilling, twittering came
To mate and nest on rafters which
Sway with the wind, hang in the air;
And from the birds at last learned not to care.

But the cold murderers move again
Towards the ruin I made my home.
Tumble and break, my cracked words, then,
Knights like the boulders on the beach
Break on their heads, though you'll make no breach,
Batter their armour when they come.

Bankrupt

Living above his means for all those years
He had no choice but in the end must honour
The world that honours every gay pretence;
Feasted rich friends for fear of poverty
And when his creditors called must turn them into debtors
Who'd count it gain to drink at his expense
And lend him more: hard cash and flattery
To keep the party going.
                              Long they'd thought:
"Fear too can fix a firm economy.
Here's one so set in weakness, count on him;
If move he must, will take such care of comfort,
He'll never feel the change — and nor shall we.
True, he looks haggard, but can face no mirror,
Is growing lean, but dare not know his weight."

It was his conscience dunned him, while they fawned
Though without cause as yet they sensed betrayal.
From street to street he dodged it, and they followed,
Remarking this chair was new, that picture gone,
The room more crowded and the carpet thinner;
Yet wine and wit flowed freely as before.

At last (removals make us) he could laugh again
Unprompted by their faces and, alone,
Prepared to pay his ransom, vanish from that city.
"But lest in vain I shed sweet vanity,"
Because the cure could breed a worse disease, he prayed,
"Salt the dry crust and keep the sour fruit pure.

To queens once exiled, my dear guests a while,
But reinstated now, I'll send no humble greetings,
Hoping despite myself for crumbs of favour.
Yet when forgetfulness is my discipline —
Which, granted strength enough, I'll not relax —
Still I'll need wealth to keep a sole friend faithful,
Such peace as will permit me to recall:
Moved by whose grace into a dingy house."

After Christmas

Gone is that errant star. The shepherds rise
And, packed in buses, go their separate ways
To bench and counter where their flocks will graze
On winter grass, no bonus of sweet hay.
The myrrh, the frankincense fade from memory:
Another year of waiting for the day.

Still in his palace Herod waits for orders:
Arrests, an edict, more judicial murders,
New taxes, reinforcements for the borders.
Still high priests preach decorum, rebels rage
At Caesar battening on their heritage
And a few prophets mourn a godless age.

The Magi in three chauffeur-driven cars
Begin their homeward journey round the wars,
Each to his capital, the stocks and shares
Whose constellations, flickering into place,
Must guide him through a vaster wilderness
Than did the star absconded out of space.

The golden thread winds back upon the spool.
A bird's dry carcass and an empty bottle
Beside the dustbin, vomit of goodwill,
Pale streets, pale faces and a paler sky;
A paper Bethlehem, a rootless tree
Soon to be stripped, dismembered, put away,

Burnt on the grate ... and dressed in candlelight
When next the shepherds turn their flocks about,
The three wise kings recall their second state
And from the smaller circle of the year,
Axle and weighted hub, look high and far
To pierce their weekday heaven that hides the star.

A Child Accepts

"Later", his mother said; and still those little hands
Clawed air to clutch the object of their need,
Abandoned as birds to winds or fishes to tide,
Pure time that is timeless, time untenanted.

"Later", she said; and the word was cold with death,
Opposing space to his time, intersecting his will.
He summoned the cry of a wounded animal,
Mindless Adam whose world likes crushed by the Fall,

But suddenly mended his face and far from tears
Grew radiant, relaxed, letting his hands drop down.
"Later", he sang, and was human, fallen again,
Received into mind, his dubious, his true demesne.

"Later", he played with the word, and later will envy
The freedom of birds and fishes for ever lost,
When, migrant in mind whom wind and water resist,
Here he must winter in body, bound to the coast;

Or, not all his "laters" past, perhaps he'll know
That the last releases: reversed, his needs will throng
Homeward to nest in his head and breed among
Those hidden rocks that wrecked him into song.

Woman at a Window

She opens wide the window into Spring,
Abstracting sunshine from a dirty wall,
A dog, a housefront, makes it plausible;
Waits till, provoked, the travelled breezes tell
The vaguest reminiscence of a smell
That's neither tar nor cabbage; before long
Sifts seasonal music out: a blackbird thrills
Above the buses and pneumatic drills....

She veils her vision, wonders at the year
Clenched like a fist all centripetal winter
Now suddenly relaxed, a tapered hand.
Imagined buds explode, the pavements ring
With turmoil of a secret burgeoning;
The city reels and cracks. She leaves it there,
Leans on the sill and launches on the air
A golden boat, a keel to cut the tide,
Sail to the breezes yields her billowed hair:
And all is ocean....

                    Oh, but she cannot ride
Those reefs, the roof-tops, and so near to land
Feels age and gravity, deflects their laws,
Creates an orchard in the window-box
Herself a shepherdess whose flocks may graze
Between the blossoming trees....

                         A door-latch clicks,
The neighbour's. 'Shepherd? Shepherd without sheep,
Farmer who ploughs and sows but may not reap,
True metropolitan.' And all is lost,
A room her pastoral island, stalks and sticks,
Last year's geraniums shrivelled on its coast;

No wilderness even, but the world of clocks,
Each breath a tick.... She pulls herself together,
Dreading his chime, forestalls him:: "Lovely weather!" —
No need: he's gone. But she, grown penny-wise,
Drinks a last draught of daylight, weans her eyes,
Closes the window, fastens it, withdraws.

London Idyll

Twelve houses fell, twelve gardens broke their bounds
Before the lovers, tempted by these fronds,
Brushed by these rambling branches, could transgress
The traffic's laws and stumbled into peace;
Bedded on grass, felt the green light grow dimmer,
The yellow light grow brighter, but recede....
Or walking here a clerk surprised the summer
Fierce in its narrow cage and, half afraid,
Dreamed his way back to boyhood beasts and flowers,
Translated into dream the screech of cars.

Here whitethroats build their nests, a nightingale
Often at early dawn strikes dumb the owl.
And here — a dole of colour to the needy —
Are poppies, buttercups for all to pick;
Or dandelion leaves: a muttering lady
Braves bricks and brambles daily for their sake.
On Sundays round a parliament of mothers
Small girls make daisy-chains or look for feathers,
Snail-shells, dead butterflies and beetles' shards....

Because twelve houses fell, now timid birds
Return to London and the lovers lie
Among tall ferns in deep tranquillity,
Hidden at nightfall in those bushes where
For hours on end the schoolboys play at war.

Man in a Garden

Creation's monster, metaphysical man
Across the garden moves his soft machine,
Propelled by timeless fuel, caught in time,
Changing, unchanging, mobile, half at home ...
His legs in Croydon, head for Eden bound,
Between two stars he tills the promised land.

A budding snowdrop beckons to his eyes:
"As flower in soil, so mind in body grows,
Wept by the primal dark" ... He tastes the weather,
Sweet on the tongue, loosening his lips to gather
Breezes like manna, but his lungs expel
Polluted vapour, warm and personal.
He listens: blackbirds fluting ... pigeons talking;
But in his entrails hears a time-bomb ticking,
Planted at birth, set for the mocking hour.
Screaming, a sea-mew hurtles through the air:
"Birdsong is praise because a bird can die;
We do not leave but take the world away,
The world that's in us, falling when we fall:
Almost we dare not live our lives at all."

And still he digs, digs in his grievance there,
Long after dusk; digs till his mind is bare
Yet in its bareness holds one metaphor:
"Stars in the dark and out of soil a flower."

A Wreath of Thistles

For Jesse Thoor

I

His laughter cracks the ceremonial cup
I'd empty for the parting of our ways;
Old wine of grief repetitive death still draws
From one deep vat for lingering friends to sip.

But look: he skips to trip my slow feet up,
The jester yet among those hierarchies
He lived in raving loneliness to praise;
Prances and hops to stop me with a quip.

Then lend me spirits, Jesse, to make fierce,
Pungent and harsh this potion for your sake;
No pander to the palate, make it pierce
And purge as did your curses — till they quake
Who to such violent rage provoked your mind
That like a blinded bull it charged the wind.

II

No, let them be. He's left the maze behind,
His vision mended and the circle full.
Let all things be. He would not ... I recall
How still one pin would fail him as he planned
A lifelong absence from the taint of land,
Wrecking the borrowed ship he hoped to sail,
Its primitive tackle made unworkable;
Wasting his cargo: gifts, but contraband.

He must have known what nightmare hatched this dream,
The metropolitan horror, exile he began
When first the hoardings lurched him into shame,
The clang of tramcars set him verse to scan.

He's launched his vessel. Let his enemies be.
He must have known how final was the sea.

III

He lived a metaphor; and so do we:
To crown the stalk; but grew so straight, so pure,
There could not long be soil to feed the flower
This side of madness, death and poetry.
Now as before I neither praise nor pity
The pride of withered leaves that proved us poor:

Transplanted there, his blossoming is sure,
And if I mourn I blame his constancy.

And yet I blame that wrenching of the roots,
His exile into anarchy; and mourn
The simple craftsman murdered in our streets,
Whose ultimate song was of a King's return —
Who, caught in wires he once had helped to twist,
Forgot the password and was judas-kissed.

IV

I hear him challenged, eager to resist
Human antagonists; and see him cower,
For ever vanquished by no visible power,
Interrogated, tortured and dismissed,
Interrogated, tortured.... Then, at rest,
Fashion his offering, a golden flower,
Or — voices, choices banished for an hour —
A silver chalice for the Eucharist.

And last of all I see the circle full
But for one journey's arc: I see him buy
A single ticket to his funeral,
Driven, but by no plausible urge, to die
Three wars away, where once his ancestors
Herded the goats and felled the mountain firs.

V

Pure glass and mercury which no image blurs
I'd let him rest who was so restless here:
Restless because a mirror, still and clear
Beyond its plane of moving metaphors.
But forced to render much besides the stars,
He stops me now to whisper in my ear
Tales of such tremors in the atmosphere,
No stars remained but whirled like meteors;

And will not rest; and will not let me rest,
But walks the streets in daylight, and at night
Peers from behind the hoardings to protest
That ghosts are wrongs not even death can right,
Unwilling loiterers who cannot pass
Till the last image fades within the glass.

VI

Then to the devils of his long distress
I turn again, beg them to let him go.
Louder than ever, jeering, they answer: "No!
We do not hold him, but the wilderness
He cannot leave, still raging at our voices.
What respite he will grant us, we bestow;
Nor shall detain him when he deigns to know
The garden — closed to us — walled for his peace."

And now they drown his outcry, hide his ghost.
Crowds like machines have crashed and mingled where
Last week I saw him stand. Projectiles whir
And whistles shriek. His face, his gestures lost,
Lost his last gust of laughter, I give up.
Acid, not wine, flows from the broken cup.

Travellers

For Edwin Muir on his 70th birthday

Some travel to lose their way; the glib and loud,
Boasting their bag, experience, in miles and days.
From sea to sea they roar, from coast to coast,
From lover to lover.
All that they praise is their own bloodstream flowing,
All that they rage at the benzedrine of the blood,
Faster than mind, their zest and their undoing.
Bored by the flora, they do not learn,
But alienate, lay waste what they discover,
Trapped in the machinations of their quest;

Can conquer but not colonize; roam but not explore.
Now climb a high peak, now dive deep for corals,
Now hunt a beast no living man has faced —
In the wrong season, with the wrong gun.
Brought close by chance to the one answering shore,
Hot hungry eyes they fix on it unseeing
While the ship moves on;
Remember no home and never return.

Another in the cabin's lamplight quietly
Construes the country where he has not been,
Waits for the envisaged bay to realize,
Easily lands and thinks his way
To a familiar city, pre-possessed.
All, all he recognizes; every tree's position,
The shapes of bridges, colour of local stone,
Moods of the sky and mode of each bird's flying;
From faces, gestures, words overheard retraces
The legend of his trials, his acquittals:
Reads how he was not wise nor brave
Till seven times shipwrecked, seven times saved,
And could not act and could not see
Till seven times blinded, seven times healed,
Battered into identity.

River Song

Not proud to row but glad to glide
Leave the certainties of earth,
Leave the doubts of earth and ride
The dimpled surface of this tide,
Element of Love's own birth.

Cygnets, ducklings do not know
What purpose launches them on glass,
How wide and long the currents flow
In the muddy bed below,
But reflected, unreflecting, pass.

Haphazard as convolvulus
Wind your thoughts, apply your hand,
Like these fluttering flowers trace
Mad patterns on the mirror's face,
Lightly glide and lightly land.

Bread and Butter Letter

To Philip and Barbara Rawson

Bread is the fields of wheat
Where partridges creaked in flight,
Faint hum of day-time tractor,
The fidgeted drum of night;
Butter the mushroomed pastures,
Meadow and muddy patch,
Parched where the clumps and the mounds are,
Sodden in hollow and ditch.

And water: the shallow river
With willow, lily and rush,
Then the sudden pool, no wider,
Though deep as diver could wish.

These are not you — nor yours
To keep or to give away:
This barn you did not build
Nor saved the roof from decay;
Yet its ruin's pattern grew fertile
When the skeleton pierced your gaze
To be more than thatched in thought —
To leap alive from your eyes.

As from ridge and furrow we gather
The spirit behind the face
And lovers even must look for
Their love's true dwelling-place,
Praising the site of your tenure
I praise both mind and thing:
Their marriage, from which all beauty
And all creation spring.

May garden, orchard and meadow,
Cornfield, river and pool
Nourish your art and prove
As ever bountiful,
Lest the abstract cities wither
That primal intergrowth
Of outward form and inward,
Levelling all into death.

May your bread be fields of wheat
And the dual pastures requite
With dual blessings your labour,
No daemon darken your site.

Under the Lime-tree . . .
(From the Middle High German of Walther von der Vogelweide)

Under the lime-tree,
By the heath,
Where with my well-beloved I lay,
You can go and see —
Pleasant both —
Flowers and grass we broke that day.
Where the forest meets the dale:
Tandaradee!
   Sweetly sang the nightingale.

Here we were meeting;
But already
My well-beloved was waiting there.
Such was his greeting,
Gracious Lady,
That ever since I've walked on air.
Did he kiss me? Yes, and well:
Tandaradee!
   Look how red my lips are still.

With the wild flowers
There my love
Made a lavish bed for me;
This bed of ours,
Should you pass above,
Will make you laugh most heartily.
By the roses you can trace —
Tandaradee!
   Where my head lay in that place.

Had anyone seen us
Lying there,
(God grant none did!) I'd be ashamed.
What passed between us
Is our affair,
Never to be known or named
But by us and one small bird —
Tandaradee!
   Which may never breathe a word.

Dialogue

"Tell us again of love and death,
Opposed, that we may picture both
Who cannot think them separate.
Death a mere empty frame we hate
And only love
At one remove:
So giddied by the turning wheel,
We need a mirror, loss, to see the loved one whole."

"Never again, since she
First breathing on the mirror hid
The macrocosmic mystery,
To leave us lost; till newly centred, grown
More partial, we should need
No other loss to prove
The wholeness of your love,
Nor any quickening discord but our own."

Mathematics of Love

The links are chance, the chain is fate,
Constricting as Hephaistos' net
Which to the smiles of gods betrayed
Two bodies on a single bed,
So tightly knit, the truth was plain:
One multiplied by one is one.

Subtracting lovers who retort
That what chance coupled, choice can part
(As if mere effort could relax
The clutches of a paradox)
At last to their amazement find
Themselves the dwindled dividend,

Deep in that hell where Don Juan
Knows he has added names in vain
Since all the aggregate is lost
To him, not widowed but a ghost,
While those bereaved of one possess
A minus greater than his plus.

True love begins with algebra,
Those casual actors x and y,
Nonentities whose magic role
Is to turn nothing into all,
To be and not to be, to mate:
The links are chance, the chain is fate.

Emblem

Only for love of love
High up this hunter shot
And missed the snow-white dove;

Then, descending to the plain,
Entered a pitch-black wood
And, blindly, shot again.

For the sake of the dove, of mountain sunlight and snow
Deep in dark woods he seeks a wounded doe.

Early Love

I

Hot in cold armour from his moated youth
He ventures out, less ignorant of death
Than of the temporal town's complexities,
Whorl, criss-cross and ellipse. Of love he knows
A peak long wondered at, disdains the slopes
Because a stranger yet to all mishaps
But headlong thought's abysses, hell in dream.
Now far from both the boundaries of his home,
Garden and moss-damp forest, he must brave
Ambiguous ways, the heart's alternative,
Moderate heights to climb with bleeding shins
And where he treads, the clatter of small stones.

II

Nothing is single there, and nothing pure:
Mind mixed with flesh, as animal with flower,
As flower with rock; and all dissimilar.

Nymph to his satyr, Psyche to his ghost
She lures him to division, at her cost:
(Darkness was daylight when the nightly god,
Nameless, illumined Psyche: dark, he glowed
Until to light his radiance was betrayed.)
No master, in the darkness of their tryst —
Meeting unlit by moon or memory —
He falters, gropes, and falls; she fades away,
Dark as the night, in unreality.

(A nymph, more weed than woman, water weed,
Bends to the current, fashioned to be swayed,
Blossoms above, her floor the river bed.)
No diver yet, he drags her image down
To drown it in that depth; back in the sun —
Too bright — he blinks and, inwards, dives again.

III

Back at the start
After the partial journey,
   His lack increased
By every landmark sighted,
   Poorer by far
Than at his first departure,
   He counts the lights
Indifferent eyes had charted,
   The lamps and stars
That leave him loss-benighted.

   A station built
Of soil's and sky's negation,
   An empty frame
Where grimy stillness strangles
   And shrill din stabs
Diminished meditation;
   In nerve and bone
Low tide of long delusion,
   Back at the start,
His partial destination.

IV

Night-flowering plant surprised, in memory
Her image grows complete. From root to flower —
Cool flame whose fire is water, earth and air —
His mind affirms her, darkness joined with day.

All one to Psyche, sunlight, lamp and moon
Shall not estrange her lover; well he knows
The tryst's illuminated mysteries
And knows a diver proves no depth undone.

Bounded at last, his station waiting over,
He'll reach the relative streets and in them find
His landmarks all assembled, all contained,
Far light reflected in the central river.

Terrible still that city, but for love's
More vivid seasons: muffled the years rotate,
Lives intersect, their clash, their mergence mute,
And in their midst a hidden axle moves.

Based on its murderous rhythm music heals:
Tune, hands and mastered instrument reconciled
In silence, out of silence he can build
His personal architecture, sound its walls.

There — nymph a house for Psyche, flesh for ghost —
Within his monochrome fierce colours burn,
His glacier melts to moss and moss in turn
Suffers the transmutation of slow frost.

Spring Song in Winter

Too long, too long
I gathered icicles in spring
To thread them for a melting song;
And in midsummer saw the foliage fall,
Too foolish then to sing
How leaf and petal cling
Though wind would bear them to the root of all.

Now winter's come, and winter proves me wrong:
Dark in my garden the dead,
Great naked briars, have spread,
So vastly multiplied
They almost hide
The single shrub to share whose blossoming
Blood on cold thorns my fingers shed.

Narcissus

Not he was beautiful, nor yet the other
Whose lustre guarded darkness on the pool —
Too much himself, too near to him for love —
But somewhere in between
Its image-haunted surface and the bed
A face grew beautiful and approved his love.

At first she would not come,
As if afraid of his or the other's face —
The other's it must be, for him she loved —
Then, as he waited, suddenly was there,
Such longing in her eyes as his for her
But inaccessible always,
Her lips beyond his reach, even her outstretched arms,
Though once he felt the touch of her fingertips,
Unbearable in that stillness, and could not stay.

But what he fled from questioned why he fled:
Where, when she came, was he, his daylight double?
He whom they said he loved
And gladly would have loved if love allowed
Such easy self-completion
As between stalk and shadow would be natural,
These rushes and their complement on the pool.
No, like the water-lily's leaves he lay
Too near the would-be mirror of himself,
Leaving no space for comfort in self-love,
Full day above, no light but hers below.

That other, then, must blur
And vanish back into himself when she
Gathered and drew him down into the dark
And in the alien element he saw
Her streaming hair, a nymph's, and not the other's.

Likeness there was perhaps; and yet no more
Than if his sister — like him to a stranger
But not to him who used no looking-glass —
Outgrowing all his memories and his grief
By change in death had learnt
To hide behind a lovelier woman's gaze.

Now from that gaze he fled and could not flee,
In heavy half-sleep nightly must repeat
The waiting and the meeting, till the touch
Of icy finger-tips shivered his flesh awake
Or plunging through her stunned him into sense.

To venture back seemed best; the silence loud
In daylight, and his double there to taunt him
Until he dared to look.
A moorhen shrieked; far off an eagle swooped and struck.
A dragonfly rattled faintly, dipped and for a moment broke
The surface of his frailty, rippling the other's face,
So that he smiled, though still the other stared,
His eyes two troubled pools within the pool.

Now, lingering, almost tenderly for once,
Narcissus took his leave, dismissed his double,
Entered those pools and sinking, sinking left
All thought of day behind him,
Could hear no sound, forgot to feel the sun,
Grew cool as water, one with water, flowed,
Slowed down when from a single pool his eyes
Diverged once more in halflight, then moved on
Towards the darkness where two points of light
Fused with himself would quench him and be quenched ...

Then he remembered: motionless on the bank
He'd left his body, motionless the other
Watched him and aped him there;
He turned about to end that mockery,
Rose up while she, receding, grew distinct;

Seeing her whole, he loosened, she rose up
To meet his fall half-way.
Clasped in her arms, entangled in her hair,
Eyes, lips and body fast, Narcissus drowned.

* * *

Strange, but the only witness, a young girl,
Crept from her hiding place on the opposite bank
To swear she'd seen Narcissus bend his head
Over his own reflected self and kiss
None but the pool's cold mouth,
Rise on his arms, slide forward and slide down,
So slow, so quiet and so natural,
She had not stirred until the surface closed,
The last small ripple vanished.

Why had she hidden there? She would not tell,
But said again: as natural, as complete
As water-irises and their complement on the pool
Only more beautiful in that symmetry
Because Narcissus still, and more than flower;
And yet not quite Narcissus:
For poised above his image on the water,
Too much himself, he'd left no space for love,
Remote from her as heron, crane, or swan,
Rooted in his own stillness like a flower.

An Unnecessary Visit

How I came to the place, I don't remember.
Like one on a pub-crawl in a foreign city,
Guided by those who know.

Suddenly I was there, deserted by all my guides,
Flung from a river-drifting drunkenness
Into those crowded confines, cruelly bright;
Sealed off from the city's flux and her stillness
As never in workshop, night-club or basement room,
Concert hall, prison or crypt.

Puzzled at first, seeing my look of pity,
They stared in silence: "Who might this tourist be?
Angelic emissary? No. Nor simple spy.
One from the lukewarm regions rather, sent
By learned institute or university
To note our habits, tabulate our torment ...
Out of his depth, has veiled his arrogant eye."

So now they brawled and bawled, half deafened me,
Played leapfrog, squeezed and scratched their sores,
Fencing with red-hot pokers, scored by the scars
Their foils probed open, shrieked out the other's gain.
But at a sign from one lean inmate, ceased,
Rigis as he approached me:

                    "Well, I'm blessed!
A temperate type dropped in on us," he hissed,
"What's more, an anthropologist! —
No, don't deny it. Why, we're flattered.
I should have thought your welcome made that plain,
A warm, a rousing welcome, you'll admit.
And drop your bedside manner. We've no use for it.

No need to look pained. No need to look depressed.
A bit of a rough-house, eh? As if it mattered.
'Inhuman', did you mumble? Of all the rot! —
Enlighten the stranger. Tell him the answer, boys."
In chorus they responded: "We like noise!"
And then, fortissimo, "We like it hot!"

As if to prove their freedom, unprompted they dispersed.
Each to his fire and intricate equipment.
A chemistry class, I thought, but saw no master;
And thought of cows come to the milking shed,
But missed the whacks and shouts.

             Watching their work,
I moved around till nausea made me pause
Near one who held his left hand in the fire
And with the test-tube in his right hand scraped
The sizzling flesh away.

             "Ah yes, we burn,"
He answered when I questioned him, his glance,
Intent but calm, never once raised towards mine,
"With a hard gemlike flame. And in that urn —
No, not the refuse bin for trash the fire disdains,
That urn of pure white alabaster — place
The pure white ash, all that remains
After the ultimate metamorphosis
Of gross corporeal matter. This —
At once the end and product of my pains —
A messenger whose origin and identity
We lack the means to trace
Daily collects and — so I trust — delivers
Where the white lilies grow that feed on it.

Sir, when you leave us, forget the coarse demeanour
By which the unsociable communicate,
Their play uproarious because their work is silent,
Their language lewd because their thought is rare.
Write of the lilies only — so white, so pure,
Our gaze could not endure them, who at best
Serve to enrich the soil of a garden for ever walled."

Even while he spoke I saw his neighbour creep
Up to the pure white urn and shake its contents
Into a dust-pan, which in turn he emptied
Into the refuse bin.

Memory choked my protest.
"Thank you," I gasped, "thank you for every word.
I shall recall your candour and your trust
When in my mind the bloody wounds are blurred,
The din's an echo and even compassion numb."
Then, longing for empty streets, I hurried out.

By twos and threes I climbed the dingy stairs,
Flung open the front door and

                    there,

A fond and faithful moll patiently waiting
Yet again at the prison gate,
Stood she who by the laughter smouldering in her eyes
Keeps lit the hellfire of my own undoing.

A Gardener Explains his Absence
from the Flower Show

If you hope to excuse me, burn these lines unread
And with an angry laugh dismiss the lapse
Of one who was always forgetful. Or blame my laziness
And recall that every spring for days I defaulted
Listening to other men's bees in the bluebell wood,
Aimlessly trespassing there without the gumption to poach,
Too morose to picnic.
Add, if you must, that later, but not in mushroom weather
I'd stray into meadows no more my own
Where only grass is various, the wildflowers are common and
    meagre.

So much truth I owe you. But guess no further, friends.
What I forgot was more than the occasion,
What I omitted more than May demands
Or all the summers left to me will mend.

September it was that sanctioned my defection.
Soon after my last attendance it all began,
When the first leaves fell and the first apples followed.
Unaided they fell on a windless day,
Their falling a kind of stillness.
And I tried in vain to think of the flower show,
This year's, next year's, any year's past or to come,
New hybrids ever more gaudy, their neutered blooms
Ever more swollen and frilled.
Then in the fulness and death of my garden I knew
That never again the soil I tended would bear
Flowers for comparison, foliage for competition,
The half-real progeny of image and will.

I neither hoed nor dug, sowed nothing, planted nothing,
Left trees and shrubs unpruned, removed no withered stalks.
If still at times I succumbed to the human fury,
Provoked, despite myself, into the outworn habit of war
By rebels once quelled, now boasting impunity,
With my bare hands and nails I tore at the nettle roots,
Ripped up the sere ground elder.

Not real enough to create, not real enough to destroy,
What peace could I defend, against what enemy?
In the growth and decay of my garden I heard
The single voice of the sparrow-hawk and his prey,
Life and death indivisible, terror and joy;
The voice, it seemed, of a single bird
Whose dual affirmation blessed
Equally the worst and the best,
The worst as prelude to the best,
Pure silence that received them both.

All winter I hardly stirred; but to survive the cold,
Burned every stake and seed-box, beat down the trellises
And salvaged wood from rusted implements.
On earth grown hard I walked without a care,
At the blank sky directed a blank stare
Until I felt the hidden fire
That's neither passion nor desire
And without fuel glows when heart and mind are bare.

April came.
Young lilac bent to the breezes, but did not break.
Gales came in time, breaking old branches,
And slowly the garden changed.
Still the soil was rich. Indifferent I watched
Rare pansies revert to heartsease,
Mallows grow tall and fat as hollyhocks.

But through brambles and briars the lilies bore
Their waxen petals unscathed —
The white, the orange, the purple and golden-streaked —
Flowering as never they did when no creeper encroached on
      their site,
Beyond gain and loss at last on a bitter day.

I look up at the roof:
The martins' mud nests are empty.
A butterfly flaps damp wings and drops on the sodden lawn.
Mingled scent of leaf-mould and chrysanthemums
And the late quinces coldly ripening
Tells me the circle's closed;
Tells me I'm free to plant and sow again if I please,
Plant and sow what I please for the coming year.

Shall we meet again?
Almost I answered: no,
Afraid there was nowhere to meet
But where blind men compete for a paper prize.
Yet "a man must live", you would say; and indeed he must.

So look out for me, friends, where the meagre wildflowers
     grow,
Or — "a man must eat" — at the market gardener's show,
Among cabbages, carrots and peas;
Not the monstrous pumpkins, plain fruit of moderate size.

Almost I thought it was otherwise:
That the years were void, unhallowed the days and the hours
Till the Lord of atoms breathes on our broken dust;
Till on a bed of flowers unnamed
Another Adam lies
Rubbing his vacant eyes,
To fill them and name what he sees.

But "accept, accept" was the cry of the stricken bird,
Accept the silence; it approved his cry,
Intolerant only of the human word
Which rising falls and falling seeks to rise,
Lusts after self-eternity
And more than once, self-stricken, dies.

Accept the hawk and the gale that strikes as swiftly,
Snapping the laden branch;
Speed of the adder's fangs, the adder's tongue.
Or time that lurks in the seed and lies at the elm-tree's core;
Long trance of the spider before
Her paralyzed body uncurls to feed the spider-wasp's young.

Making do with the catalogued lilies, shrubs that the ancients
     knew,
I'll go and look for a spade, whet what's left of the scythe.

Horseman, Pedestrian, Dog

"Soul, I protest. The shade of ancient trees,
The secret walks, walled garden and peacock's cry,
Dew on the lawns and the silence greater than these,
My heritage I gave up; and moved to the shanty town
That by subtraction of such properties,
Tethered to death and bare your peace I might own.
Soul, I protest. A dog's my conscience now.
His host and slave I rot in the hovel of pity,
Though with concrete, tin and plaster incessantly
I patch and build."

      "Time's acre of mud you plough.

Why, false pedestrian, if now you're shamed
By a mere dog, anxiety,
Call on the fierce antagonists you tamed
When you were young to smother
That grovelling cur who would not let you be.
If your arm's feeble now, win peace by policy,
Pitting one devil against another."

"You underrate the dog.
Pride and ambition, lust and cruelty
Will make a pact with him and pounce on me,
No less afraid to crush so loathed a creature
Than you to crush a spider or a frog.
In that half-animal
They sense the wild beast's fall,
Wolf, jackal, man all mingled in his nature.

An obstinate lout can bend a stallion's will,
Stuck to his back until
One centaur king they clear the thickest wall.
But if a cur snaps at the stallion's heels
A riven centaur reels
And in the ditch dog, horse and rider sprawl.

Dog is the first to rise;
Then the great riderless horse who'll leap no more.
Still rigid, though unhurt, the rider lies,
Never once turning to forestall
Deeper and longer coma, his disgrace.
He does not stir before
A limping whimpering mongrel licks his face,
Fondly to stay with him. Long after he'll recall
That seal of love, the spittle on his eyes.

Soul, set me free. In dreams I knock on the door
Of my own lost house, and they turn me away,
Fell the limes and the chestnuts, butcher the deer.
When I wake the dog's on my bed — and feeds on me,
Begs me to barter for a marrow-bone
The framed mementoes, ghosts of my possessions.
What next shall I renounce?"

                    "The lie
Of your renunciation that is none,
Crooked resort of the heart's lechery.

Longer perhaps you should have lain
Dazed in the ditch; till you were whole
By virtue of that resting-place,
All memory of your horse and house,
Because a cur could love you, gone.

Well, there's another way — or more.
Whether you drag on crutches or
Fly for the joy of flying, where
Truly you are I too shall be.
Stylites' column, Xerxes' throne,
Neither is low, neither is high.
But you were gross in poverty.

Dismiss the mongrel, then. Pick up
Your boots and spurs and riding-crop;
They'll do, if only you use them well,
Means to an end you guess. Now call
The horse that never could stray far,
You, his sole master after all,
Being so nearly motionless,
Get on your animal's back and ride
To the proud house the tall trees hide."

Epitaph for a Horseman

Let no one mourn his mount, upholstered bone
He rode so cruelly over bog and stone,
Log, fence and ditch in every kind of weather;
Nor glibly hint those two came down together:
A horse fell dead and cast his master down,
But by that fall their union was undone.
A broken jade we found, the rider gone,
Leaving no token but his cold clean gear,
Bit, reins and riding-crop for friends to gather.
None but a beast's remains lie buried here.

III

Of Time and Place

1957-1964

She

At last, at last she has come back to me
Dreamed in disproof of love's topography,
Real contours we explore
Only to lose in dreams, in dreams of her
Who is no girl or woman
But luminary, moon that was before
The moon herself was human;
Who, heavenly body still, and featureless face
Needs neither lips nor fingertips to stir
With supersensuous telegraphy
Her farthest antipoles, while she
Shines cold, demure.

Homage to the Weather

A tide, high tide of golden air.

Where, till this moment, were the bees?
And when no hum made for the honeysuckle,
Fumbled,
Became a body,
Clung and drank,
Spindrift, disowned, the petals hung,
And wait, let go was what the summer meant.

A corner of the garden, ivy on broken slats,
A branch with orange puffs: buddleia globosa.
Between two gusts a flood of golden air,
Mere hush, perhaps, abeyance — but the bees
Clinging and drinking.

Walls they brought with them: black courtyard in Paris,
A bit of marble, tumbled, dust on leaves,
A goldfish pond, the traffic not remote,
Audible, yet excluded;
Flowering tree or shrub in any weathered city,
Walls to contain a quietness, a quiver,
Fulfilment of the year, bees to be stilled.

Between two gusts, cold waves, the golden tide.

Tides

To wake without fail when milk bottles shake in their racks,
Scrape one's face in the morning, every morning,
Take the same route to work and say 'good morning'
To the same row of scraped or powdered faces —
I cursed the roundness of this earth, I raged
At every self-perpetuating motion,
Hated the sea, that basher of dumb rock,
For all her factory of weeds and fishes,
The thumps, the thuds, the great reverberations —
Too much in rhythm; jarring, but by rote.

The metronome it was in my own head
That ticked and ticked; caged cricket in my head
That chirped and chirped until I had no ear
For syncopation, counterpoint of stillness
Beating against all music — of the sea,
Of birds and men, of season and machine,
Even of cricket and of metronome.
In silence I learned to listen; in the dark to look.

And unrepeatable now each morning's light
Modulates, shuffles, probes the daily faces
Often too suddenly different, like the street,
This weathered wall re-pointed, that new one cracked,

Apple trees that I prune while I forget
The shape of last year's boughs, cankered or grown,
And where that stump is, one that died in blossom;
Forget the hill's curve under the aerial masts.

No, wheels, grind on; seasons, repeat yourselves,
Milk bottles, rattle; familiars, gabble 'good morning';
Breed, hatch, digest your weeds and fishes, sea,
Omit no beat, nor rise to tidal waves.
Various enough the silences cut in
Between the rock cave's boom and the small wader's cry.

In a Convex Mirror

A stately room — chaise-longue and easy chairs,
Old jugs on carved commodes, a clavichord,
Three landscapes, minor eighteenth century,
Against the pale grey walls; and all in half-light,
The street being narrow, the houses opposite tall,
Each with a room like this — a waiting-room.

Sunk in a chair, quite still, a waiting man
Who stares into a classic composition
Heavily framed above the mantelpiece.
A streak of grey, myself in miniature
Against pale pink upholstery, exhales
Invisible smoke; and slowly moves one hand,
Ten minutes only here, half lost already,
Half vanquished by the furniture, half absorbed,
But for the ticking of a clock would yield
All his defences, call the blur delusion.

But 'trumpery' now I mutter, jump up to break it,
Command my legs to walk, jerk my glazed eyes
Out of this glazed anachronism's eye,
And hear my name called; going, look once more:

A classic composition; nothing stirs.
One little streak of grey that matched the walls
Removed, but in that half-light far too faint
To leave a gap, and soon to be replaced.

The Body

Blue sky. White sand the wavelets lick and leave.
Alone his body struts, alone lies down.
Spiced with what springs, tautened in what tart winters,
It crouched and ran and leapt and climbed and hung,
Pulled at the oar, to exquisite horsebacks clung,
Rippled and swelled and sweated, flew on skis,
Braved currents, breakers, basked on how many shores.
The fruits and wines of every region fed it,
Beasts, wildfowl, fishes and more curious fauna
Its narrow bulk displaced. To the best winds it went,
Now noon, now morning sun for blending of its colour,
Now high, now low for cordials of good air.

None stalks it now to win or to admire,
Nor yet to kill. Of its own prime it dies
Where still he waits for her who in one glance will gather
Those foods, exertions, weathers, distances,
In his true landscape recognize her lover,
Each dear perfection answered in her eye.
Night took them all; smothers indifferently
Flesh of whatever tint, complexion, shape,
Abetting not the goddess but the woman,
Carnivorous mind more lithe than ever body was
In turning alien substances to gain;
Love, the sole acrobat, all limb and maw.

The sun's eye dims. No eye but his looks there.
A blotted contour, cold, his body struts
On greyish sand the wavelets lick and leave.

A Horse's Eye

I did not stop today at the five-barred gate,
Did not wait for the old white draught-horse at grass,
Unshod, unharnessed these many years; walked past,
Preoccupied, but something made me look back:
Her head was over the gate, her neck was straight,
But I caught her eye, a wicked, reproachful look
From one small eye slanted in my direction.
What right, I defied the old mare, what right had she
To expect caresses, the grass foolishly plucked
For her hanging lip, her yellow, broken teeth
And her great historical belly? Of course she's a relic,
Curious now as the old white country house
That stood empty and alluring in the wood behind her
Till converted into flats — not as useless as she,
Who will never become a tractor! What farmer would care?
Only some town-bred, animist, anthropomorphic rambler
Or week-end motorist looking for what he's lost.

I walked on; but plainly her glance had spoken to me,
As an old peasant's might in a foreign country,
Communicating neither words nor thought, but the knowledge
Of flesh that has suffered labour in rain and wind,
Fed, relaxed, enjoyed and opposed every season.
Broken now. Close to death. And how differently broken
From that Cossack mare the clumsiest rider could sit,
All speed and nerve and power that somehow responded
To the faintest twitch of a will less tense than her own!
Wild nature still; her eye no peasant's eye,
But lava under glass, tellurian fire contained.

As for the old white mare, her reproach was just:
Because she was too intelligible I had passed her by,
Because not alien enough, but broken as men are broken,
Because the old white house was converted now,
The wood about to be felled, a tractor chugging
Beyond the hill, and awkwardly she trotted
On legs too thin for her belly bloated with age,
Alone in her meadow, at grass, and close to death.

Arctic Explorer

Whether dog will eat dog, likes boot leather frozen or boiled,
Whether walrus will prey on whale — the white or the grey? —
Or only on seal — the bearded or common? —
And is able in time to digest the clam swallowed whole;
Whether man can eat dog that has eaten the poisonous liver
Of polar bear, and wake up to indulge in a salad
Of sorrel and purple saxifrage after a breakfast of auks:
These were a few of the questions which if he did not answer
He probed as far as he could with his naked senses,
Knife-blade, bullet, harpoon, and the pain that probed him.
Fossils too he brought back and notes anthropologists noted —
The Eskimo's fear not of narwhal but bumble bee —
Temperature charts and rough maps of the nameless
        mountains,
Cures for frostbite and skills never dreamed of at home,
Never called for, either, never again to be used.

Brought back the knowledge that all his knowledge was loss;
And worse than loss, betrayal. Of musk-ox, of eiderduck?
Of gentle Eskimo? Soon to be anyone's game?
Them and more. Of the hard land unlocked by his loving
To procure for the pimps of empire another whore.
And wished he had brought back nothing, not even his body,
Left it to wolf or to fox, to the poppies' ravenous roots
Or only to glacier and silence, the diamond moonlight in
        winter.
Stayed there, died there in the first hard act.
Greater cold now he longed for, wider, more blizzard-swept
        skylines
For ever receding, crevasses more cunningly opening
And blindness the consummate vision, white, white to the
        point of blue,
Ice in his veins, and the snowlight burning to ice in his head.

Bird Watcher

Challenged, he'd say it was a mode of knowing —
As boys in railway stations neutralize a passion
By gathering ciphers: number, date and place —
Yet keeps no records of his rare encounters,
Darkly aware that like his opposite
Who no less deep in woods, as far out on the moors
Makes do with food and trophies, hunts for easy favours,
He trysts defeat by what he cannot know.

'Goldfinch' he says, and means a chirping flutter
From stalk to stalk in early autumn meadows,
Or 'oystercatcher', meaning a high, thin cry
More ghost than bodied voice, articulation
Of the last rock's complaint against the sea.

And wooing with his mind the winter fieldfares
Has made a snare of his binoculars,
For lime and cage and gun has longed in secret,
To kill that he may count, ravish despair
And eat the tongue that will not speak to him,
Though to the wind it speaks, evasive as the wind.

He grows no lighter, they no heavier
As to his mode of loving he returns,
Fixed in the discipline of adoration;
Will keep no pigeons, nor be satisfied
With metropolitan starlings garbling their parodies.

The boy's cold bride will yield, too soon and utterly,
Never these engines fuelled with warm blood,
Graced with peculiar folly that will far outfly him
Till in one communal emptiness they meet.

Old Woman

She seems to drift, but talks against the current,
Observes a daffodil on the present bank
But strains toward its double of another spring
Not truly seen when seeing was too easy,
Her will less flexed against the drowsiness
Of dragging limbs, so near now to the sea,
With all the weight of eighty-six years to keep
From sleep that would be drowning.
So late she dare not drift, her work unfinished
As when a servant girl denied her sleep
To show the guests out, clear the table, polish
The silver cutlery, she dared not rest
Till almost night and morning drudgery met,
The silence was perfection.
And even now it's tidying keeps her up —
To talk her dead alive, sharp-tongued, cut through
Crust after crust of dirty circumstance
To set one legend free —
His whom by self-negation she upheld
Till the cold killers drove him from her tending
And out of memory,
Beyond her ken and kinship, wrenched his face.
Round, round she seems to whirl; but making, mending,
Laboriously retraces
A broken circle, his blurred lineaments;
Laughs as he laughed, and curses as he cursed
That she may come at last to where his voice gave out
Too soon, in the absurdity of death,
Smile as he smiled there, but less bitterly,
And, her work done, be still.

Blind Man

He can hear the owl's flight in daylight
When, surprised, on silky wings it shoots
From a low perch; and by the open window at night
The stag-beetles blundering in the hedges
On the far side of the meadow. Geese half a mile away
Honk near as hooters of swerving cars
And do not alarm him. Indifferently he awaits
Dogs that he feared when they slunk or bounded
Visible at him, as if in his carapace
Of darkness for ever secure from harm,
Wombed and housed and coffined within a wound
That has hardened to armour. The screech and the hum
Blend and subside in a resonant quiet,
Shapes he has fumbled to feel fall back
Into unbroken space when his hands forget them,
And still are present in his no man's land;
Above the nightmare tamed by light's extinction
The apple that hangs unplucked, grown fabulous.

Man of the World

Strange, but he cheats his master
Who without fail or stint pays in good notes and coinage,
For ever seeking to convert that currency
Into the sleep of metals and of stone.
Malachite, agate, lapis lazuli
Weigh down his papers; his eyelids are heavy with sleep.
Not bonds, not journals, line his inmost walls
But rows of books, his graveyard of choice minds,
Asleep until he rouses them,
Images fixed on paper, canvas, wood,
The disc engraved with voices of the dead,
Not flesh or leaf, time's pasture, but porcelain, ivory, bone.

Sleep is his wages; hatred of sleep
And fear of what might break it,
Sickness or slump,
The clumsy servant's duster,
Instruments of the retribution that will shatter
All that belies his means, outlasts his ends —
His master's ends, not his:
Though on a nightmare's back, he gallops into truth,
Though but to crash or stumble, rid of the glazed disasters
That were his juggler's toys,
Feel the raw grain and jagged crust of earth
And wake to serve his master loyally.

Because

To the child's 'why?' parents invent an answer,
To adult man's, scientist and philosopher
Their long cacophonous chorus of 'because'.
How mind abhors a circle! Let there be laws!
A schoolboy knows effects must have a cause.
All know it but the wise man and the dancer,
Tautologists who as they turn are still,
Find every virtue in a vicious circle —
The serpent's mouth that bites the serpent's tail —
And are because they are because they are.

Variations on an Infant Theme

For Richard

I

"I love you and I love me" —
So you chanted at the age of three,
Happily truthful then
And effortlessly wise
As never you'll be again
Till, one more graduate in the school of lies,

You choose the dangerous descent
More difficult by far
Than the same way when, guided, roped, cajoled
To every known foothold,
One of a crowd you climbed, and lay content
Not with yourself — loving not what you are
But what they were and deigned to let you be,
Gathered into their own self-flattery.

On ledge and peak beware
Of too delicious air,
Dazzle of quartz light, glitter in the scree.
Though by negation now you will progress,
Chasms of loneliness,
The terror that in one fall
You will lose all
And, shattering, disprove
That ever your self's mirror held the shapes you love,
Go down, go down, my son,
Back to your starting-place —
Sheer on the sheer rock face,
Bare mind in world's embrace,
Your pride and your conquests undone.

II

Hazy you'll leave the hut where climbers eat and sleep,
With fingers half awake at first will clutch
Dream rock, real rock, only to rest again
On the bare boards, self-love, the bed of all your loves,
Base of your search for vistas or alpine flowers,
Whatever phantoms inwardly you collect.
Love makes you real, makes real the ghost of flowers
And flesh that would be ghostly but for love.

Guessed in the dark or limned in naked sunlight,
All, all can vanish though you climb no more,
Fences, walls are in good repair and your thoughts
Only on dwelling dwell now, possessed by possession.

105

To night oppose night, or dawn may catch you staring
At a garden suddenly withered, leafless in June,
Your pasture land for ever veiled in mist;
The bolt you slide into place have nothing to guard
But its own echo subsiding in an empty house.

III

"I love you and I love me" —
What in yourself you are will be
Your outer journey's map and paradigm;
Only what in yourself you love
Grow as you grow, move as you move.
Out-climbing self, the loved one you'll out-climb;
Too long at rest, her limbs immobilize;
Purblind, will read your blankness in her eyes.
Self-centred is the light by which you see,
That makes you real, and real reality,
Ripens your crops and measures out your time:
All seasons and all weathers may that light approve.

Conformist

Branded in childhood, for thirty years he strove
To hide the scar, and truly to believe
In the true fundaments of that commonweal
Which once had outlawed him beyond repeal,
And with true awe, true gratitude, true love
Would gaze upon the incorruptible guard
Before the gate — the keeper of his peace
Who in mean streets could live anonymous...

Until conformity brought its reward:
A crested, gilt-edged card. The great gate opened,
A pair of stiff lips cracked and let him pass
Into those halls his half-life's dreams had deepened;

And out again...to breathe the ownerless air
Night sky transfigured, lucent, fresh and clear
After the ceilings puffed in emulation.
His own place found at last; his own self found —
Outside, outside — his heritage regained
By grace of exile, of expropriation.

What had he seen, ushered behind the gate?
The dress and furniture of his own terrors,
A glittering medal pinned on his own wound,
And, at the heart, an empty hall of mirrors.

Healed now, of health, unmasked, of honesty,
In, out again he passed, with one smile met
The questioning eyes of flunkey, potentate,
Townsman and guard shrunk to complicity,
All one to him at one with every station
Since none was his, nor ever now could be;
Come late into the freedom his from birth,
To breathe the air, and walk the ownerless earth.

The Moment

Trapped in the whorls of a conch time roared.
Eye, mind met walls,
Could neither enter nor rebound,
The moment lost in plotting for the act.

Sleep cracked the shell,
In lidded eyes unlocked the cells of light,
Undid no knot long fingered,
Traced no new shape, nor any sign but this:

Morning, the slanted beams
Through low dark boughs and the bunched leaves of bushes.
A streak of lawn illumined? Yet
It was not grass or grain of wood and leaf
That held the moment whole. It was the angle:
Sunlight, and how it fell.

Instead of a Journey

Turn like a top; spin on your dusty axis
Till the bright metal shines again, your head
Hums and the earth accelerates,
Dizzy you drop
Into this easy chair you drowse in daily.
Sit there and watch the walls assume their meaning,
The Chinese plate assert its blue design,
The room renew itself as you grow still.
Then, after your flight and fall, walk to the garden
Or at the open window taste return:
Weather and season, clouds at your vision's rim,
Love's whims, love's habitation, and the heart
By one slow wheel worn down, whetted to gladness.

Quince and Blackthorn

Trunk hard and ridged, more fit for hedges
If more than trunk, not by a curious marriage
Disarmed of spikes, lopped and tamed in an orchard
To bear this wealth of delicate boughs cascading,
Flounced pink, downed gold, devoured by parasites
Strange to his grain's potential, fostered disapproving.

Crest lithe and light, the weather's dancer
But for the bitter moods for ever rising
From his dark roots and the dank clay beneath;
Fearing each leaf-fall, fruit-fall, yearly diminished
Not for his sake, to swell the festering humus
That breeds and buries, feeds and chokes unheeding.

Gardener indeed, who grafted quince on blackthorn,
Binding two kinds, two minds, by one sap mellowed,
Lifelong divided, indivisible lifelong in labour
For fruit not like the sun's gold or his aborted berries
Gratuitous, never learned the art of undoing,
From wounded fibre exacts the blossom whole!

Trunk hard and ridged, more fit for hedges
But for this wealth, her delicate boughs cascading
From his dark roots and the dank clay beneath;
By dint of wealth, downed gold by one sap mellowed,
Grown more than trunk or his aborted berries:
Crest lithe and light, the weather's dancer.

Security

1

So he's got there at last, been received as a partner —
In a firm going bankrupt;
Found the right place (walled garden), arranged for a
    mortgage —
But they're pulling the house down
To make room for traffic.

Worse winds are rising. He takes out new policies
For his furniture, for his life,
At a higher premium
Against more limited risks.

2

Who can face the winds, till the panes crack in their frames?
And if a man faced them, what in the end could he do
But look for shelter like all the rest?
The winds too are afraid, and blow from fear.

3

I hear my children at play
And recall that one branch of the elm-tree looks dead;
Also that twenty years ago now I could have been parchment
Cured and stretched for a lampshade,
Who now have children, a lampshade
And the fear of those winds.

I saw off the elm-tree branch
To find that the wood was sound;
Mend the fences yet again,
Knowing they'll keep out no one,
Let alone the winds.
For still my children play
And shall tomorrow, if the weather holds.

Errors

A short-wave station gabbles and hums —
The newly filled tea-pot.
Turtle doves coo in the corner —
Something vibrates as I type.
Outside, a mechanical saw —
Guinea fowl screeching.
A pheasant's repeated hoot —
Cars on the new road.
I bend and smell tom-cats —
Blackcurrant bushes;
Mimosa —
Meadowsweet.

I appoint my two eyes judge,
Sole upholders now of the decencies
Of reason, identity, place,
Yet from Thames to Riviera
Am wholly transported:
Meadowsweet to mimosa,
The blue-white-silver, yellow-tufted trees
On the mountainside
Long unvisited, never missed.
And the daily hill gone.

Old Poacher

Learned in woods
As troubadour in words,
Delicate as a troubadour's lady,
Killer of does grown doe-like
In nostril, ear,
Lithely, gravely he stalks
His quarry
That will never know death.
And men stalk him.

Only a hawk cries
Above the clearing;
Robin and blackbird are still.
It is the hawk will cry
Till his eye meets
The man's eye
And silent he dips over oak-tops
In flight that is not fear
But hunger's cunning.

Fearless, wily, the man
Listens:
For dog's pad on moss, dry leaves,
Brushed fern, torn bramble,
Panting breath, cough,
Squelch of boot in trough;
Or cropped grass,
Nibble on low hazel bough,
Scuttle of hoof, claw.

And feels again
The thorny joy
Of his great indifference:
To have almost forgotten death
In the woods, in hunger's
Mastery over fear;
With senses grown
Reliable, reliant,
And a man's mind
To savour the sense —
Hunting, hunted, both hawk and deer.

Omens

1

The year opens with frozen pipes,
Roads impassable, cars immovable,
Letter delivery slow;
But smallpox from Pakistan
Carried fast from Yorkshire to Surrey,
And no lack of news:
In the Andes a landslide
That buried a town;
In Dalmatia, earthquakes;
Bush fires around Melbourne,
Cooking wallabies, koala bears.
In the Congo, another rebellion;
In Algeria, random murders on either side;
Paris a playground for thugs.

2

The milk our children drink may or may not be poisoned
By last year's fall-out, no longer part of the news.
Our earth may be shrinking, expanding
But was found to contain great cracks
That will doubtless widen even without our help.

3

Amid such omens
How do we dare to live?
Brashly building, begetting
For a town besieged,
Crumbling, patched again, crumbling
And undermined?

4

Deeper I gulp cold air that not too suddenly kills,
Greedily drink with my eyes the winter sunshine and clouds,
The old white horse in the meadow
Green again after snow.

Next year I shall see no meadow, no horse.

Anachronisms

From a London sequence

I

Where the paint cracks, refracted in his gaze
A red geranium in a window box
Of any terrace house, means more than meadows;
A single flame kindled against the grime,
Element of his kind, means more than sunrise
Blazing as ever on bare indifferent hills.

A lighted window three rungs of rooftops higher,
London at dawn the broken man reflects,
A hint of summer frocks, brightness contained,
Soon to explode in sparks of multicolour
When, decomposed, housefronts assume their numbers,
Daylight identity their scattering ghosts.

Time in the park, packed in the traffic's rumble,
Pattern of light and shade the tall trees make,
The dead friend met in the street, or nearly met
Where sharpest oddity has its duplicate —
Only what men have broken and men repaired,
Time, light and landscape mastered, he approves.

A red geranium against familiar grime,
At the grey moment that allows refraction,
Paint that was greener, and carnations, were they?
Gathered against the day, he turns, prepares.

In tube train, street
Through faces, voices he travels,
From smooth to rugged landmark,
The misty crag, the ditch-fed willow lost
In near or distant exile.
Sucked into eyes, explores
Glazed images:
A patio here with plants in ageless pots,
There, tanks over cobbles,
Tall houses shaken,
Clotted blood on tramlines.
In this watery blue
An English village,
Aerials on raw roofs;
Small monotone of bullfinch
On the hill stripped
Of orchards and elms.
That great moustache
Over tight lips
A laurel hedge imposed
On concrete fence posts, the new plot;
Beyond it, a gardenless row,
Back yards of stevedores, packers,
Coal fire abandoned one night
To smoulder on beneath the nightly cinders...

III

Jolted, he fumbles for his tie:
What street, what perished house am I?

What brawls, what yells engraved the scars
Deep in my hearing?

Horns of what obsolete cars
Driven towards what hollow rendez-vous?
What smells of refuse wafted through
My first awakenings?

Too many faces.
I cannot remember them all.
Too many voices.
I fall and fall.

IV

Roves again, and is held,
Pledged by one answering glance
To the man from Ghana
Adrift in Europe, his white stiff collar
Rimmed with London's grime,
Carrying pamphlets, and letters addressed
To the heads of churches and sects,
With a second class railway ticket
And not enough cash for a meal.
"A good will mission — you understand?"
Then laughs: "And seeing the world"
(Shrunk, they taught him in Ghana,
To the dimensions of love).
Off to Paris, then Cyprus.
Meanwhile, what ought he to do
Which way should he travel?
How send on his trunk?
What language, please, do they speak in Vienna?
And their religion? And that of the Yugoslavs?
What papers are read in England?

116

Should he write to The Times or The Daily Mirror?
And what should he look at in London? —
Well, what till now had he seen? —
A room in a lodging house
Open to coloured men,
A room shared with friends from Ghana.

On a mission,
Interdenominational —
'Inter-demoni-national', he seemed to pronounce it.
Seeing the world:
Bowler hats in London,
Eyes politely averted.
Railway officials in Paris
Not even polite
To strangers in dirty collars
With second class tickets,
No cash for tips or a meal.
Received by political prelates,
Dismissed with phrases, more letters
And the promise of grants —
The man from Ghana,
Pitting good will
Against perplexity,
Sowing the seeds of union:
Pamphlets, crumpled, damp
In the dustbins of Europe.

V

Horns of obsolete cars in a different country,
A city razed, rebuilt;
In half-sleep heard the incomprehensible din.
Across the yard, upstairs, the drunken lesbian
Was beating her meek wife.
Nightmare and day were one; drives to the hardware shop
Soft soap in barrels that smelled of despair.

And the bleakness of hardware was everywhere
Till I came to the lake, and the water dragged me in,
Dragged me down to drown like a pebble, glibly;
And was rescued in time, saved for the world of hardware.

Who was that boy,
And who the man, the soldier
In a different country again,
Well fed, well housed, well looked after among the ruins
By a homeless man, Ukrainian, his batman briefly
In an idyll of mountains, forests and lakes
Where an Austrian ex-prisoner of war
Let his wife to a British cook for tins of American beef
And a homeless Yugoslav in his camp
Hired men with smuggled gold
To murder homeless Yugoslavs in their camps.

What self was that,
Riding a Cossack mare (requisitioned, her owner
        machine-gunned
When we honoured our obligations
By sending his trainload of traitors across to the Russian Zone)
Over ice, through knee-deep snow, in pine-needled air
Or on pine-needle track to the Alpine glades in summer?
Boats too we had, a boathouse by the lake,
And in I plunged again, though not to drown
But to kill time that was an interim
Between the death of one self and the next
Between the end of one war — and the next?

VI

Heels click
Soles shuffle
Engines hum,
Brakes grind
Drills throb
A lorry rattles.
Eyes veiled with haste,
Low voices lost in the drone.

He walks.
He halts
And hears the silence of London
Built into walls,
The old and the new,
Buried beneath the humus,
Beneath the sycamore's roots.

Silence holds
The city together,
Absorbs the thrust
Of piston and wrist.

Clouds race over all,
Factory,
Terminal,
Park where the lovers lie,
Hospital ward
And black canal.

The sycamore's branches push
As though to crunch
Window panes,
Light bulbs.
Ivy winds
Towards the sycamore's trunk.

Vacant lot.
From the garden
Cry of a child at play.
The silence holds it,
Detains in remembered rooms
The friend long removed.

High noon.
Wind in the sycamore's leaves.
New faces, new voices,
Clouds that race over all.

VII

They come back to me now,
Each bungled death, half-death,
Each bungled love, half-love,
Each reawakening, rebirth,
And they who were part, are part
Of the one self, the many selves,
Of the one place, the many places,
The one time, the many times —
Are found again, and are lost,
Are not what they were, what I was,
And are all that I am.

The Witness

1

Over the telephone
From a call-box, ice-floe, raft
Comes a voice:
My name is Roberts. Yes, in a way you know me,
At least, we have met. Remember the Shetlands?
Perdita Roberts? Well, she's my mother.
They're abroad. May I call?
Good, I'll be with you in half an hour.

2

The voice a man's.
The forgotten name a child's
With eyes coal-black as the woman's
Who put him down to play Brahms,
The Rhapsody,
In a cottage that smelled of wet wool.
Walked on the moors with her later
Towards the flickering lights,
Heard the sea roll, the sea boom
Beyond the barbed wire,
In winds one lay back on
Or charged head down;
Resisting the winds, the sea,
For time's sake, human time's,
Though out of time we walked
Away from cottage and camp, from the child asleep.
Had almost gone down in that sea
Avoiding submarines,
Kit afloat below deck,
Even the crew sick.
Before long was posted south,
Leaned on the railing, looked,
The sea calm for once.
Was she there on the quay,
The child in her arms?

121

3

Twenty years old, as I was then,
He comes into my time
With no claim on my time, a stranger,
To talk of his time and mine, recall
A house in London, a bus-stop,
The taut threads linked once again, to snap —
Till now, the stranger come back,
Strangely akin, as though
The nearly drowning had been

A death as good as another,
An island, neither's home,
Had been a meeting-place
Where ice from ice had drawn
Fire, and the flickering lights
Like sunbeams had seared the moors,
His time and mine, this room
Were no more than walls raised up
Against the winds and the sea,
The sea, the winds a whisper
Loud in his ears and mine,
And we, on separate ships,
One leaving, one returning,
In neither's time going down.

Oxford

Years on the Gothic rack:
Bells crashing down on green water,
Lashing the tree trunks for growing,
The meadows for lying flat.

And the flushed girls laughing
At calf love.
Planting banderillas
That itched and dropped, but to burn —
All moved on, moved on

Not where the arches would fling them,
Not to a cloistered garden
Nor yet to the riverside,
The willows, the weeping willows,

To pins and needles in armchairs,
Shrilling of telephone, doorbell,
A well-mannered print or two
Of towers, Gothic, black
Against trim foliage, blue sky.

At Fifty-Five

Country dances
Bird calls
The breathing of leaves after thunder —
And now fugues.
Modulations "impolite"
Syncopations "unnatural".
No more clapping of hands
When moonshine had opened their tear-ducts
Or fanfares clenched
Heroic nerves —
But a shaking of heads:
Can't help it, our decomposer,
Can't hear his own blundering discords.

As if one needed ears
For anything but chit-chat about the weather,
Exchange of solicitude, malice —
And birdsong, true, the grosser, the bouncing rhythms.
Uncommunicative? Yes. Unable
'Like beginners to learn from nightingales'.
Unwilling, too, for that matter —
To perform, to rehearse, to repeat,
To take in, to give back.

In time out of time, in the concert no longer concerted.
But the music all there, what music,
Where from —
Water that wells from gravel washed clean by water.
All there — inaudible thrushes
Outsinging the nightingales, peasants
Dancing weightless, without their shoes —
Where from, by what virtue? None.
By what grace but still being here, growing older?
The water cleansed by gravel washed clean by water.

Fugue, ever itself —
And ever growing,
Gathering up — itself,
Plunging — into itself,
Rising — out of itself,
Fathoming — only itself
To end, not to end its flowing —
No longer itself —
In a stillness that never was.

For a Family Album

Four heads in one lamp's light
And each head bowed into peculiar darkness,
Reading, drawing, alone.
A camera would have caught them, held them there
Half-lit in the room's warm halflight,
Left them, refused to tell
How long till that lamp was broken,
Your hair pinned up or cut or tinted or waved.

I cannot even describe them, caught no more
Than a flash of light that ripped open
The walls of our half-lit room;
Or the negative — a black wedge
Rammed into light so white that it hurt to look.

124

Leave this page blank.
You'd neither like nor believe
The picture no lens could have taken:

Tied to my rooted bones
In your chairs you were flying, flying.

IV

In a Cold Season

I

Words cannot reach him in his prison of words
Whose words killed men because those men were words
Women and children who to him were numbers
And still are numbers though reiterated
Launched into air to circle out of hearing
And drop unseen, their metal shells not broken.
Words cannot reach him though I spend more words
On words reporting words reiterated
When in his cage of words he answered words
That told how with his words he murdered men
Women and children who were words and numbers
And he remembered or could not remember
The words and numbers they reiterated
To trap in words the man who killed with words.
Words cannot reach the children, women, men
Who were not words or numbers till they died
Because ice-packed in terror shrunk minds clung
To numbers words that did not sob or whimper
As children do when packed in trucks to die
That did not die two deaths as mothers do
Who see their children packed in trucks to die.

II

Yet, Muse of the IN-trays, OUT-trays,
Shall he be left uncelebrated
For lack of resonant numbers calculated
To denote your hero, and our abstract age?
Rather in the appropriate vocabulary
Let a memorandum now be drawn up —
Carbon copies to all whom it may concern —
A monument in kind, a testimonial
To be filed for further reference
And to circulate as required.
Adolf Eichmann, civil servant (retired):
A mild man, meticulous in his ways,

129

As distinctly averse to violence
As to all other irregularities
Perpetrated in his presence,
Rudeness of speech or deportment,
Infringements of etiquette
Or downright incompetence, the gravest offence;
With a head for figures, a stable family life,
No abnormalities.

Never lost his temper on duty
Even with subordinates, even with elements earmarked
For liquidation;
Never once guilty of exceeding his authority
But careful always to confine his ambitions
Within the limits laid down for personnel of his grade.
Never, of course, a maker of policy,
But in its implementation at office level,
Down to the detailed directive, completely reliable;
Never, perhaps, indispensable,
Yet difficult to replace
Once he had mastered the formalities
Of his particular department
And familiarized himself with his responsibilities
As a specialist in the organization
Of the transport and disposal of human material —
In short, an exemplary career.

III

Words words his words — and half his truth perhaps
If blinking, numb in moonlight and astray
A man can map the landmarks trace the shapes
That may be mountains icebergs or his tears
And he whose only zeal was to convert
Real women children men to words and numbers
Added to be subtracted leaving nothing
But aggregates and multiples of nothing
Can know what made him adept in not knowing
Feel what it was he could not would not feel —
And caged in words between their death his death

No place no time for memory to unfreeze
The single face that would belie his words
The single cry that proved his numbers wrong.

Probing his words with their words my words fail.
Cold cold with words I cannot break the shell
And almost dare not lest his whole truth be
To have no core but unreality.

IV

I heard no cry, nor saw her dying face,
Have never known the place, the day,
Whether by bullet, gas or deprivation
They finished her off who was old and ill enough
To die before long in her own good time;
Only that when they came to march her out of her human
        world,
Creaking leather couch, mementoes, widow's urn,
They made her write a postcard to her son in England.
'Am going on a journey'; and that all those years
She had refused to travel even to save her life.
Too little I know of her life, her death,
Forget my last visit to her at the age of nine,
The goodbye like any other that was the last,
Only recall that she, mother of five, grandmother,
Freely could share with a child all her little realm;
Recall her lapdog who trembled and snapped up cheese —
Did they kill her lapdog also, or drive him away? —
And the bigger dog before that, a French bulldog, stuffed
To keep her company still after his early death.
Three goldfishes I recall, one with a hump on his back
That lived for years though daily she brushed her fishes
Under the kitchen tap to keep them healthy and clean;
And how she conspired with us children,
Bribed us with sweets if we promised not to tell
Our father that she, who was diabetic,
Kept a pillbox of sweets in her handbag
To eat like a child in secret —

When neither could guess that sweets would not cause her
    death.
A wireless set with earphones was part of the magic
She commanded and freely dispensed,
Being childlike herself and guileless and wise...

Too little I know of her wisdom, her life,
Only that, guileless, she died deprived
Of her lapdog even, stuffed bulldog and pillbox of sweets.

V

And yet and yet I would not have him die
Caged in his words their words — one deadly word
Setting the seal on unreality
Adding one number to the millions dead
Subtracting nothing from death dividing nothing
Silencing him who murdered words with words
Not one shell broken, not one word made flesh.
Nor in my hatred would imprison him
Who never free in fear and hatred served
Another's hatred which again was fear
So little life in him he dared not pity
Or if he pitied dared not act on pity;
But show him pity now for pity's sake
And for their sake who died for lack of pity;
Break from the husk at last one naked grain
That still may grow where the massed carrion lay
Bones piled on bones their only mourners bones
The inconceivable aggregate of the dead
Beyond all power to mourn or to avenge;
See man in him spare woman child in him
Though in the end he neither saw nor spared —
Peel off the husk for once and heed the grain,
Plant it though he sowed nothing poisoned growth;
Dare break one word and words may yet be whole.

Treblinka

That winter night they were burning corpses
And from the bonfire, flooding the whole camp
Flared purple and blue and red and orange and gold,
The many colours of Joseph's coat, who was chosen.
Not cold for once we at the barrack windows
Blinked and listened; the opera singer,
Unafraid for once, found his full voice and gave it
To words, to a music that gushed like blood from a wound:
Eli, Eli…his question too in whose name
Long we'd been dirt to be wiped off, dust to be dispersed —
Older than he, old as the silence of God.
In that light we knew it; and the complaint was praise,
Was thankfulness for death, the lost and the promised land,
The gathering up at last, all our hundred hues
Fierce in one radiance gathered by greater darkness,
The darkness that took our kings, David and Solomon
Who living had burnt with the same fire;
All our hundred languages gathered again in one silence.

To live was the law; though to live — and not only here —
Was a hundred times over to spit in our own faces,
Wipe ourselves out of creation, scatter as dust,
Eat grass, and the dung that feeds grass.
The grass, the dung, the spittle — here we saw them consumed,
Even these bodies fit in the end to yield light.

Back in a room in a house in a street in a town
I forget the figures, remember little but this:
That to live is not good enough: everything, anything
Proved good enough for life — there, and not only there.
Yet we lived, a few of us, perhaps with no need but this:
To tell of the fire in the night and briefly to flare like the dead.

Between the Lines

Yesterday, just before being transported back to prison, I
committed a terrible gaffe. Two people came out of the
interrogation room. One of them, tall, elegant, speaking
a very cultivated French, looked so tormented, as though
about to break down. I asked him with concern: "Vous
ont-ils malmené?" "Qui ça?" "Mais eux." He looked at
me, shrugged his shoulders and walked on. Then the
German sentry said: "But that's a Gestapo man."
                                     Prison diary of E.A. Rheinhardt
                                     Nice, 22 January 1944

Later, back in my cell, back in the thick stench
From the bucket shared with three men whose dreams are of
    flesh
Not for beating or fondling but eating, I laugh, laugh
As never before in that place, even when gorged with a treat
Of gift food from a parcel. For then I would drift
Away from our common attrition by hunger and filth
To my garden, those hardly believable flowers
That may open again though I am not there to tend them,
To my bed and, almost, the mingling of bodies in lust,
And would hate the voice that clattered into my refuge
With a curse or a joke. Now they are close to me,
My fellow victims, decent men at the most,
Blundering into death as I do, devoid of a fury to hurl
Against our tormentors, the furious burners of books
Numb with the icy need to know nothing, be strong.
I laugh, laugh at their strength, at our feebleness
And laughing feel how one I could not believe in
Allows me to blaze like his martyrs, consumes me
With love, with compassion; and how the soul
Anatomists cannot locate even now will rise up
When my turn comes to blunder again, when I cry
To the killer who cracks my joints: "Je te comprends, mon
    ami…"

Meeting

for Johannes Bobrowski

"Here I was born —
On the other side of the city,
Back in the murdered years;
Neither here nor there I'm at home,
On my way,
In search of the place."

"Here I'm at home —
On the shore, I look eastward
Into the murdered years;
Where the lake recedes from sight,
And farther,
I come from there."

And yet, we stand here together,
The water is quiet, our eyes
Fix on it, meet on it, rest —
On neither side of the city,
In a year that's alive.

After Attica

1

Rock, rock and the sea.
Fishermen mending their nets
In the shade of tall houses
Locked up when the captains died out,
Galaxidi fell silent,
The olive trade passed it by.

At Itea now
The great barrels are filled,
The ferries loaded with strangers.
And Itea's fishermen sit
In the shade of low hovels
Mending their nets.

2

Three vultures glide
Towards Parnassos
From the olive groves of Amphissa;
Over temple, theatre, stadium,
And the pine groves above.

The flycatcher flits
From fallen pediment
To mended pillar.
A long brown snake
Darts from loose rubble
To rooted thyme.
The holy site is a garden
For goldfinch, marigold, orchis.

Three vultures glide down
Over the valley
Where hooded crows
Perch on judas trees
To snatch the larger share.
Broken cry
Of a donkey laden with branches.
A shepherd stands in the glare,
Whistles to bell-wether, ewe,
And the lambs will follow.

Soon melted snow
Will replenish the little river
That now is an ochre track;
The swelling asphodel bulb
Will be celebrated

And, after fasting, the slaughtered lamb.
There will be dancing
To Giorgos the barber's guitar,
Neither child nor mule will be beaten
Till the women resume
Their digging, pruning, picking
That the ritual may be fulfilled.

The god who came from the sun
Has returned to the sun.
The prophetess is a cave.
The Castalian spring
Waters almond and fig tree.

The words to the song have changed.
This terrace carved out of rock
Bore a shrine, a villa, a pillbox:
Anemones bend in the breeze.
And three yellow vultures ride it
Back to the sea.

3

In halflight
Heavy with incense
Eyes blink
At unblinking eyes,
Black symmetry
Against a heaven of gold.
King's gown and shepherd's kirtle,
Green, red and blue
Pay homage to black.
Amplified in the domed silence
The humming of bees.

Scarred by earthquake, war,
Patched and impoverished
The forecourt collects
Larger quietness
Of mountains and valley.

Heavier than incense
The fragrance of blossoming laurel.
From a shallow basin's rim
Bees drink the cold spring water.
A monk on the balcony
Reads yesterday's paper.

DEMONSTRATION IN ATHENS —
Truncheon, tear gas turned
On women, old men.
Survivors perhaps,
Defenders once of these vineyards
When three hundred were rounded up,
Herded into the shambles
To pay for one soldier's death.

And now the tourists:
A café here, a shop,
Rúgs from Aráchova,
Mementoes of places missed out
Or blankly visited,
Works of art — too many —
Conceived in the camera's womb,
Undeveloped, unborn.
Their guidebooks that leap
From Oedipus at the crossroads
To our holy Luke,
Neither mention nor name those others.

So we moved our ikons
To a homely chapel,
Left to them the basilica,
Open now, and empty
Till the next coach pulls up
With click of shutters, buzz
Not of bees, but voices
Complaining of roads and hotels.

Pray for them,
Pray for eyes that blink
At unblinking eyes,
Outgazed, like us all.
That ceiling too will go
Despite our propping, patching:
May there be eyes here to blink
At the sun
And be outgazed,
Hands to water lettuce,
To tend the bees.

Woodland Lake

For E.B.

Parkland once, on the right bank of the Thames,
And the lake an artefact
Dug out of sodden clay to be wholly possessed
As the river could not be; now private beyond the design,
Moated with man-high nettles,
Scrub and bramble, ankle-deep mire, dead branches,
Fulfilled. Black crystal. Never so darkly limpid
When before leisure's decay
Keepers dredged it, a lady walking alone
In the scream of a peacock heard all her acres lie still.

Mottled with willow shade
Moorhen and mallard drift on nobody's water.
And higher, it seems, through boughs overhanging or
    mirrored,
Basking, languidly gliding,
Left behind, suspended, two golden carp,
Their bulk, their age immune, the lake's time theirs.

First Thing in Berkshire

1

I wake
To summer dawn
And the burble of thrushes,
Syncopation of sparrows' tutti
Dotting the blank air;
And blank with sleep
Almost I let their natural discords trace
A valley ruled by its river, nightingales,
Till dew and sun declare
An open contest of greens —
Water-green, leaf-green, grass-green —
Wavily, dottily dancing out of the mist.

Avallon, warble the birds, Vézelay —
No, the spaces in between;
Those meadows had no name,
The river no name but mirror
To clouds with no history;
The name of the valley was green.

2

I wake
To the interdict:
A valley, true, Thames valley,
And the thrushes burble
Where asphalt and concrete have suffocated
Mile after mile of earthworms,
The sparrows, driven from bulldozed hedgerows,
Make do with aerials,
Fight for the nests vacated
By martins that failed to return.

Every house has a name —
Moviesta, Inglenook, Karma —
Every strip of garden a use;
But uselessly on the patch I am weeding
Plop the bodies of linnets
Bored to death by the boy next door in his deadly boredom.

3

I wake
From a sleep
Duly dreamless, blank.
No collusion, the interdict said,
Of men with birdsong,
Even in dreams.
That valley the dawn proposed
Is subject now to the Council's planning,
Even in dreams.
As for nightingales,
Kindly expunge the word:
If the creature is not a fiction
It will certainly not be permitted
To disturb the ratepayers' rest.

Time to get up now, high time.
Already the thrushes, the sparrows
Have turned to vital pursuits.
Through the window, in waves and dots,
Cold air transmits reproductions
Of a crooner's recorded sobs.

The Col

Col de Castillon, Alpes Maritimes

The near sea or the far —
This blue pool glittering
Beyond the town compact on its rock,
No mast on the pool, a sparkle not of the waves,
This road a serpent, flashing
Here and there an eye, a scale
(Headlights, roofs of cars
Creeping, slithering all day long
Toward Italy, back to the coast)
Or the snake that lay crushed in the road,
Half disembowelled by tyres,
The hooting, screeching never quite silenced but when
Wreckage obstructs a bend,
The police are at work
And people get out to picnic,
Take snapshots or play with the dog
Until with crescendo of broken donkey cries
The ambulance comes for the wounded?

This peak, the two circling eagles
Known by their height, their remoteness,
Or the stony path on the col
Where stretched from broom bush to broom bush
Invisible threads attach
To our eyelids, lips and hair,
On lavender, anis, thyme,
On the droppings of goats, on carrion
Day-moth and swallowtail settle,
To look up is to stumble,
Tripped and ripped by low brambles?

The shapes of the mountains blur
As when clouds came down,
Dripping from pine and oak.
Resin it is that sticks,
Cobweb and dried blood.
Plaster from church walls

That shelter scorpions now
Like the village's other ruins,
Empty stable, gutted house.
Juice from fig and plum
Burst where they drop
Amid the run-away vines
And the stones broken loose one by one
From the terrace walls of the slopes.

The far blue pool is for postcards,
The panorama for eagles
To keep and freeze under glass.
Cloud-drops, for me, on threads,
Bitter-sweet pinecone, green
Grass that the goats pluck, warm herbs,
The pin-eyed doll's head of a praying mantis
Swivelled round to stare.

The House Martins I

Pines I remember, the air crisp.
Here, in a haze, elms I see,
Do not see, and hills hiding the river.

But the roof is generous,
Can preserve nests. And again the martins mutter
Their small-talk, daily domestic twitter
After those miles, deadly to some,
Over glaciers, over high waves.

Arrived, arrived in whatever wind,
To ride all winds and, housed on the windy side,
Warm with their own blood the cold mud walls.

The House Martins II

1

Fifteen years later. From under an older roof.
In weather blown in from the north,
With roses that rot in bud, sodden.
In a colder, windier county:
Again that muttering, on the windy side of the house.

Fluttering exits, a jerkier tacking
Than the swallows' that, flashier, shoot
Into flight from their perches indoors,
On the sheltered side,
Through a square gap in the panes
Less wide than their wingspan.
Or the swallows' homing, a headlong dive
Into familiar darkness.

Never loud as the swifts that shriek as they swoop and glide
High up in great circles, and mate on the wing.

2

Again that muttering. A muted gabble,
Low gurgle under the eaves.

The smallest words are not small enough
To record them, the martins, and their small recurrence,
Their small defiance, of more and more.

So I repeat: fifteen years later.
Here they are. Again. Still.
And can perpetrate no infinities, for comfort,
Nor mouth the metaphors that will damn my kind
The summer I see their empty nests.

Grey Heat

Grey heat, but a breeze blends
Day lily with evening primrose,
Bronzed orange with purest lemon.

Care lasts longer, and longer
The town's blend of grey,
The rise, the crumbling of brickwork.

Less long the thrust of a spade at the roots,
The blows of great hammers on housefronts,
The grey sea wave that licks the light from your eyes.

Dare look, presume to believe
The blending of day-long petals,
Momentous whim of a breeze.

The Jackdaws

Gone, I thought, had not heard them for years;
Gone like the nuthatch, the flycatcher,
Like the partridges from the bulldozed hill.
Now it was I who was going,
And they were back, or had never gone,
Chucking, bickering up on the elm's bare branches.

I forgot the changes, the chores,
Jackdaw's corpse in the water tank,
Jackdaw's nest, jackdaw's dry bones, dry feathers
Stuffed down the chimneys —
No longer mine to clear.
I heard them, I saw them again in the cold clean air
And, going, my tenure ended,
Brought in the harvest of three thousand weathers,
The soot, the silver, the hubbub on trees left behind.

Removed

Lost, the land looks away,
The light in the orchard glassy
Like the eyes of our white cat
Who before the vans came
Lay down there and died,
Leaving the last of her many litters
Unweaned in a bramble thicket,
Hair on end, hissing.
And she whom I buried there
Prowls through the high grass.

She belongs to the elm's black bulk,
Silvery green of the apple trees
And the faint wind that carries
The lowing of heifers up
From the farm she was born in;
Whose meadows are raw soil, churned,
Milking-shed, barn disused,
Gate hinges broken;
To the hills beyond it, their beeches
Huddled and bunched, a thick cloud.

Wholly now, in late halflight,
The land disowns us.
From branches a century old
For the first, for the last time
Overripe pears drop.
And tail in the air, sniffing,
Ears pricked, deaf to my call,
Out of an empty house
Into the hedgehog's, the owl's garden
Walks a white cat.

Home

1

Red house on the hill.
Windward, the martins' mud nests
Year after year filled
With a twittering, muttering brood.
On the still side, hedged,
Apples turned in on themselves
A damp, dull summer long
Until ripe. Rare hum of bees.
The two great elms where the jackdaws roosted,
Beyond them the wild half-acre
With elm scrub rising, rambling
From old roots —
Never tamed or possessed
Though I sawed, scythed, dug
And planted saplings, walnut,
Hazel, sweet chestnut,
A posthumous grove.
And the meadow's high grass,
Flutter of day-moth over
Mallow, cranesbill, vetch:
All razed, bole and brick,
Live bough and empty nest,
Battered, wrenched, scooped
Away to be dumped, scrapped.

2

A place in the mind, one place in one or two minds
Till they move on, confused, cluttered with furniture,
        landmarks.
The house let me go in the end, sprung no more leaks or cracks,
The garden ceased to disown me with bindweed, ground elder.

What's left is whole: a sketch or two, a few photographs,
A name on old maps. And the weather. The light.

147

3

Seeing martins fly
Over a tiled roof, not mine,
Over concrete, tarmac,
A day-moth cling
To a nettle flower,
Hearing children, not mine,
Call out in a laurel-hedged orchard,
I'm there again. Home.

Friends

1

Here he sits, on the red couch
As twenty years ago on the green or blue
In a different house.
And if I shouted for joy,
Look, we are here, alive,
Wrily, faintly he'd smile:
Not to have died young
Before the dream passed through
Leaving you busy,
You with children about you,
Leaving me
Wherever I may be sitting,
Walking, standing or lying,
Eating, smoking, answering yes or no
Out of the fog, into fog,
Unable to try to remember
What it was like to care
Whether and what I remembered,
Whether and what I tried —
Not to have died young
Means that the couch is red.

2

And I think of another
Who died, with children about him,
Busy always, with words
Neither song nor speech —
Such words
As the dead might use,
Had they breath to waste —
Breathed for the dead.
Between his river, his heron
And the nearest cottage, burnt out,
The hiatus, deathly distance
Bridged by his breathing.

A clavichord
I remember, never heard him play,
A tiled stove, he stoked it;
Old books, new pictures,
A good face, blurring.
A bundle of letters
I keep, the writing clear
While his hand rots;
And I hear his voice
Clearly, more clearly than
Ever I heard it there
In his room, looking
At the stove, the pictures,
His clavichord.

3

Our loyalty, old friend, is to the dark
As yet again we walk the same few streets
Past the same grimy hedges,
New cars, new dogs and glossier paint on doors,
Hardly to notice them, or how this wall has crumbled,
But talk as ever of taxes and conscription,
Small victories, small defeats.
And though for twenty-five years you have been saying,

149

What will become of us,
Too well you know it, meaning not us at all
But his regalia, or else the many things,
Real things, realia of the working day
We care about, only because we know
How poor the realm is, how mad our king.

He dreams, and abdicates,
Leaving no heir, the currency in doubt,
Crying: The King is dead. Long live dead kings —
Lords, by divine right, over dodo and mammoth,
Rulers of nettles, commanders of lava,
Defenders of icebergs adrift in forgotten gales.

Poor capital. Poor streets that still we walk.
Mad king who laughs at those who serve him
And, re-instated, longs for a larger kingdom.
We're nothing in his dream. His dream is ours.

Every-Day

Breakfast bores me. I grumble
At the dryness of daily bread,
Blaspheming forgotten gods
(Good riddance to Penates,
Lares Familiares,
Stuffed shirts of ancestors)
But their priestess too, alive
And present — thank whom.
Oh, faced with cereal packets
"Whose name may I speak?" The maker's?
And after the soup (re-hydrated
Or genuine stock) "when late we
Rest from the life of each day,
Tell me, to whom give my thanks?"
Teach me hymns to dusters,
Paeans to saucepans. But who?
Mostly to her, though, to her

Who till all begins anew
And we know in whose name she blesses,
Has ears to hear me, lips
To smile and mutter forgiveness,
Hands that can touch and be touched.

Shakespeare Road, S.E. 24

Not marble. Yet low down
Under the windows of this corner shop
A multicoloured frieze,
Crazy patchwork of little bits,
Hand-made, one man's defiance.
No picture postcards and no statuettes;
No call for them here
As in that other place
Where now they look for him,
His absence is bought and sold,

Grassily quiet now
In orchards walled or hedged
Sweeten mutations of his leathercoat,
Pomewater, costard, codling, applejohn,
Russetting too, the rare, the dying savours.
Blackbird and thrush and linnet, the same, the same,
Sing to no ear quite open,
No eye quite open dares nor lens can follow
Business the winds and clouds transact
With light, green light, half-sunbeams with the leaves.

Here, then. Look for him here
Where boys ride bicycles over rubble, skirting
A grey van gutted of its engine, dumped
Outside the Council Works;
Down a long row
Of dingy terrace houses
And, facing it, a barred and spiked embankment
Of willow herb and refuse, depots and railway sidings,

His road, and anyone's,
With relics of a sort,
The rag and bone man's horse,
The rag and bone man's wares,
Perhaps his book, patched and passed on,
Lived in, moved through.

Brixton

You can keep the newspapers:
Nothing happens for us, here.
Even the soot is old, old,
And the weeds in the cracks of our back yards
Have strayed from counties we cannot imagine.
Our windows are curtained, blind.

That old man in the white terrace
Remembers a village, downs.
We remember nothing, here.

Why the black looks, neighbour:
But for us your white would be greyer.
In the park your children and ours
Kick dead leaves for conkers.

Brass Band in the Park, South London

Siberian winds and their detonations
Deflower the rhododendrons.
Even the pigeons take flight.
But for three muffled ladies,
One shivering girl,
The chairs they play to are empty.

Such is art. Or duty, it could be, keeps
Their faces impervious, cosy
As a beatle-style boy, slouching past,
Blows them a smart rejoinder,
His mate crumples with laughter:
So much brass for a creaking polka,
Enough to make a battalion
Of great-aunts, great-uncles hop —

While in Unter den Linden
Out strut the guard, impervious
To Siberian winds, to an urchin
Guying their goose-step, so high
That a sight-seeing Russian soldier
Retreats, his jaw-bone in danger,
Even the pigeons take flight.
The chairs on the café terrace are empty.

S-Bahn

Berlin, 1965

The gunpowder smell,
The corpses have been disposed of,
The gas rose up, diffused.
Kaiser, President, Führer
Have come and gone,
The housewives in funny hats
Came from the suburbs to shop,
Came from the central flats
To litter the woods and lakes,
Gushing about 'Natur'.
What remains is the carriage smell,
Tobacco smoke and heaters in stale air,
Indefinable, changeless
Monkey-house odour
Heavy on seats as hard
But emptier,

Now that the train connects
One desolation with another,
Punctual as ever, moves through the rubble
Of Kaiser, President, Führer,
Is halted, searched and cleared
Of those it would serve too well
This winter when, signalled on, it crosses
The frontier, no man's land,
Carrying only the smell
Over to neon lights
Past the deeper snow
Around dead financiers' villas
And the pine-woods' darkness
Into the terminus
Where one foreigner stamps cold feet.

Bed Sitter

Bare but for cooker, couch,
A few books, oranges on the shelf,
A doll and a toy dog, the suitcase packed
With material for dresses. Her other possessions
Were stolen in Italy, on her way home
From a job in Baghdad. She has travelled,
On her way still though she waits here, thinking
Of jobs, of death — not by gas
Or gentle bleeding, falling asleep;
By knife-blade's, bullet's entry, rape.
Yet she wonders where else
She might have travelled, alive;
A doctor almost of this or that,
How endured being secure in this
Which rules out that. Put up with whose love,
She who loves a memory of herself
With no job, in a green light,
Wind's traffic in leaves;
Oh, yes, and a boy, the one
Who's chosen to marry the girl

With a better job. Him?
'Yes, I love him — last year' —
Cold in her beauty meanwhile,
Her body locked lest it yield
All she has to save up, for death.

New Goddess

1

Mirrors line her shrines,
Full-length, for thighs, knees
To her are dedicated.

Men? They have not been abolished.
Mirrors too their eyes
Can serve the cult

When goddess, priestess in one
She treads profane ground,
Office, pavement, shop floor,

2

Once their domain
Who now are a curious adjunct,
Useful if tame,

As poor cows to farmers once.
Oh, their god's daily tribute
Of grumbles about the cost

Of labourers, winter fodder
And vets! All those male contraptions,
Usable still

Now that farms run themselves
And what with A.I.
One bull goes a long way,

3

Though bulls will slaver, lowing,
Farmers wheedle: love.
How the goddess laughs

Back within her walls
Of pure glass,
Water whose coolness drowned

The boy Narcissus.
Love? The goddess alone
Is a surface-bather,

Surf-riding, wrapped
In her skin of latest cut,
Can dive skin-deep,

4

Keep dry and consort
With mollusc, weed, fish,
Immortal until

Time, their god's invention,
Doled out by farmers once,
Oh, as love too,

Makes heavy with emptiness
Her womb, her breasts,
And the shallows, rippled,

Drag her down, down.

Orpheus Street, S.E. 5

1

Will they move, will they dance,
These houses put up by the money-makers
For the meek, their no-men, to breed in,
Breed money dispersed now, decayed?
And the pawn shop, government surplus,
The cut price petrol station,
Dirty brick, waste paper,
Will his music gather them up?

2

Orpheus transfigures, Orpheus transmutes all things.
His music melts walls. His music wrings
A smile from the lips of killer and nearly killed.
He wills pavements to crack. He whistles at trains,
They whimper, gasp and give up. Wherever "it" sings
It is Orpheus — with it, well paid for his pains.
Grow, says Orpheus, and dog collars burst,
Tall factories shiver, the whole town swings.

3

Oh, but the traffic diversions.
The road marked World's End, The West,
Runs north and east and south,
And the policeman on duty sneers:
Never mind the direction. You'll get there.
Be courteous. Be patient. If you park
Your car will be towed away.
If you walk, louts will kick in your ribs.

4

Orpheus is peaceable. Orpheus is faithful
To the woman who was his wife,
Till she suffered a blackout, going
Down, down, where he couldn't reach her,
Where no one belongs to himself,
Far less to another. He lost her;
But loves her still, and loves everyone,
Richly paid for loving.

5

They shriek, they sob for Orpheus,
For a shred of his shirt or flesh.
He turns right, then left,
Proceeds, does a U-turn,
Turns left, turns right, turns left,
The shriek in his ears, everywhere.
He swallows a capsule, prepares
A love song, a peace song, a freedom song.

6

The smile on her face, her smile
When he questioned her eyes for the last time
And she walked away from the stranger.
In halflight he sees no warehouse
But chasms, a river, rock.
A last glint on her hair
And the cave's darkness takes her,
Silent. Silent he leaves.

7

Let lamp posts be trees for once,
Bend their trunks, the park benches
Fling out their limbs, let them fly,
Narrowly missing the sparrows.
Street and mind will not meet
Till street and mind go down
And the footfall that faded, faded,
Draws closer again in the dark,

8

Lamplit or moonlit, his deathland:
Chasms, a river, rock.
The cries of children in alleyways,
The cries of birds in the air,
And the talons, innocent, tearing.
A head will float on foul water
And sing for the rubble, for her,
For the stars, for empty space.

Teesdale

Walked up to the scar.
Walked down to the beck.
Walked on wet hay, on heather,
On limestone, on spongy grass,
Learning the shapes of tiniest lichen and rock plant,
Marsh crowfoot and meadow campanula,
The various yellows and reds of the monkey flower,
Habitat of juniper, of mountain ash,
Haunts of curlew and grouse,
The wide distribution of starlings.

Bathed in clear shallows, in pools,
In deeper, peat-coloured water.
Saw dawn and dusk, noonlight, moonlight, starlight —
Caught a snatch or two of the small-talk of place.

When the wind began to sing,
Articulate, with human voices from nowhere,
There was an end to small-talk,
Not one peewit to be heard.

When the mist came down
There was no pasture, no copse,
Only the smell of hay getting lost in moorland,
The green and the crimson moss drowning.

Wind and mist —
They took all the rest away.

Oxwich

Wide windscape: the sand moulded
As waves are, into mounds,
But higher, scalloped, rounded
To hold the heat in craters
Walled against winds.
So too birch and ash bend,
Succumb to lichen, salt,
Early stunting, decay;
Brambles crawl, lying low
To save their sparse blue berries,
Intruders here, though prolific
Farther back where the tall trees huddle
And the wind's way ends
Up against rock and the rainy hillside.

Long seascape, interlocked
With various land.
Fresh water comes down to brine
From loam through marshland to gravel
And with the lushest warbling
Of blackbird, thrush in warm leaves
Mingles a curlew's fluting
And, windblown, an oystercatcher's;
On shallow banks the footprints,
The detritus of herons, of gulls.

Discount the castle above,
Hidden, and foreign here
As campers who drink a morning
Too bitter-sweet for comfort
Though wind and rain hold back,
A jungle of weeds exhales
Earthy richness beyond the dunes.
Guests at a dangerous marriage
Daily solemnized, broken,
They walk abeyance, close
To whirlpools, to sheer cliffs,
And will not return when the fox
Leanly lopes over ice.

October

In Memory of Vernon Watkins

1

October brings gulls to London:
Shrieks from their knife beaks
Above car drone, railway rumble
Gash open a hazy morning,

2

Bare the cliff, more sheer now,
His narrow clifftop house
Who has died on the wrong sea's coast,
The garden he dug and planted,
Hedged against gales. And the cliffside path
His days and years and decades
Kept clear of bramble, gorse,
Thickening now, while the clay mud
Clogs his last footprint.

3

Peace in the Welsh hills? Their silence
Is here, in London, it fell on him there,
Tugs at words on paper,
Colours, shapes on canvas,
Pebbles, shells from the sea
Though more slowly these fade than the skin
Of a face towards winter,
The silence is in them, the silence
Is round them, it weights, it waits.

4

Lithe on the weedy rocks with prawn net, lobster hook
He studied the tides; and the tides washed in
Corpses of men, of shag and oystercatcher,
Once on the longest headland had marooned him and his
    friend
Dylan so drunk with looking, listening, breathing,

Tidelore and clocktime failed them,
Loot almost for the sea
And gulls, looters of the sea's loot,
Irredeemable riders of the sea winds.

5

The tides he studied, but caught the bus
In time to count out banknotes only to earn the time
To count out syllables in time with no clock, no tide —
Though the waves were in them, the winds and the winds'
    riders,
Cries from the sea, the silence of hills — to provide for house
    and garden,
Humanly living in time to redeem what time, whose time?

6

Gather what can be gathered. Let nothing go
On this or on that coast, Atlantic or Pacific,
Loyal even to water, to wind and gulls,
Talk with dead friends in dreams, talk with the living
Who are here and not here, their time not ours.
Let them go, let all things go, loyal to water,
Gather what can be gathered, driftwood, dead mollusc shells,
Lobster and crab and prawn to provide for the living.

7

After frost the deepest red,
Deepest gold in chrysanthemum flowers,
Chestnut leaves, when the haze lifts,
Sparrow and thrush are silent,
Above car drone, railway rumble
More faintly, shrieks from knife beaks
Here in London to loot
From land, bringing sea cries,
Seatime no death disrupts.

8

Verse is a part of silence,
He said. Irredeemable time.
Our time it redeems,
Gathers what can be gathered,
Words, colours, shapes,
Faces that fade towards winter,
The house, the garden lost;
Loyal to water and the sea's loot,
Wind, and cries in the wind.

Loach

Loam, slimy loam, embodied, shaped,
Articulate in him. The strength, the softness.
His delicate eye draws light to riverbeds,
Through water draws our weather.

In gravel, mud, he lurks,
Gravel-coloured for safety,
Streamlined only to shoot
Back into mud or merge
In gravel, motionless, lurking.

Low he forages, late,
His radar whiskers alive
To a burrowing worm's commotion,
Tomorrow's thunder;
Advances bounding, prods
And worries a quiet pasture,
Munches athwart, in a cloud.

More than loam, at times he must rise,
His need, his weakness, richly to breathe;
Will rest on weeds, inconspicuous,
But, worse, gulp air, blow bubbles aft,

Expose a belly naked and pale, transparent.
Stickleback, minnow
Gape at his wriggling, uncertain
Whether to nibble or flee.

Perch can swallow him whole.

In Massachusetts I

For G.E.

1

Crows yap in the wood. This murmur
Is chipmunks, they dive
When dead branches crunch underfoot.

I cross fields of maize,
Papery now in the wind,
Make for the farther woods —

The maple's reds and the maple's yellows
Are flames above, in the sun,
Are embers below me —

And come to a track, a clearing:
Mortuary of metal,
Motor cars dumped, a blue,
A chrome and white holding out
Against the fire of the years.
How long, till rust takes them back?

Or this homestead, flimsy, a bungalow.
This farmer scything
The purple black-berried weed
Doesn't know its name. Poison,
He says, a Pole, unfamiliar still
With all but the sandy soil
And the ways of his cattle, deep

165

In stalks of goldenrod, of michaelmas daisies;
Doesn't know his collie's breed:
So foreign, he hardly looks up.

No need for words. But this chirping,
What body, cricket or frog
Hides in the pines, what feathers,

Russet or crimson, ruffle
Over that little cry,
See me, see me, the more to be here?

2

On. A brook winds
Through the wood. Against black leaves
Russet markings on crayfish tails
Remind me. (Forward they crawled, feeling their way,
Backward they shot, blindly.)

Banks and logs I search,
For turtles —
Too late in the year.

But motionless there a beaked fish
Shines, his knife-blade flank mottled and opal-green —
Never known, never seen before.

And now, at the pond-side, my looking
Is referred to the sky,
To tree-trunks, any tree-trunks, and ubiquitous water.

Back to the meadows, then,
Silk exploding from milkweed, little rootstock, grain
Soon to be covered by snow, till I am gone,

So that merely to walk under the low sun
I am free, and pass, leaving the signs unread,
These buds too cryptic for my decoding.

On, on, to forget, unlearn it all,
Even the bluejay's name, recalled by no blue wings
Unless they flash once more in those empty spaces
Left by unlearning, by forgetfulness,
Larger each day, as I make for a dark house.

In Massachusetts II

1

In a dark house too
There is movement, a coming and going.
The bluejay's cry
Rises above the noise of a street
Where the cars are double-parked:
Blue wings, olive, grey and off-white
Of the underside not recalled
But seen, grown familiar as all
The coming and going, all
Who came and went.
To the door of a dark house
The postman brings
Words that will not be read.
Still
This yapping is crows, whether
I listen or
Am half-deaf with the buzzing,
The rattling, humming, shrilling
That turn on, turn off
By day and by night in
A house that's not mine;
Whether I write for a living
Friend or one dead.

2

And of nothing now that concerns
Him or me. Of the black pond
And quivering light, yellow
Of leaves reflected, yellow
Of leaves drifting down
To float for a while;
Of sunbeams, turning.
Of the snake,
Blackish and yellow-striped,
On the bank, head raised
From the coiled length of a body
That pulses, at rest.

There I stand, looking;
And make for no place but
For this, where
We've no business, none.
And the house, bright
Or dark,
Is not ours.

Feeding the Chickadees

To Robert Francis

1

Titmouse, tom-tit we call
Their twitter and cheep, their
Flutter and hop as now —
Their young are fledged — they flit
Through London cherry trees
And chickadees I hear
In hemlock, pine, white birch
Outside your hermit's cabin
Twitter and flutter and flit
But stop,

Perch on a twig and drop
On to your hand,
Sit and peck seed.

2

I watch them and weigh up
The cost of so much patience,
The cost in your other lives:
Merely to stand there, keep still
Year after year till they
Could feel the root of you
Grown steady, your branching arm
Clawless, and down they came
Not to be blessed, to feed,
Yet by their feeding to bless
You with their heedlessness,
You with a counterpoise,
A meeting of your need and theirs

3

For a moment. Seemingly. Then
Oblivious they flicked their wings,
Left you to gaze into green
Stillness,
Alone with your lasting need
For that which touched is tainted,
No longer itself. Which known
Withdraws from the knowledge, flies higher.
Needs no witness, no praise.
Needs only to be
Or, untampered with, die.
For that you spend your days,
Into that gaze on your hill

4

So near Manhattan, vertical thrust of steel
Per ardua ad astra,
The horizontal thrust of knife and fist
Down in the streets, down in the underworld,
Waste paper, yesterday's war news run amuck
Through evening processions to the supermarket
And, nights, the blackness beyond the glare,
Wilderness not of nature setting in
Beyond the subway entrance, the park's edge,
Sleep to be bought with drugs or Magic Fingers,
An office block's flat roof ledge and on it after dawn,
Sucked in through grilles with gases and used air
The shriek, the shriek, the shriek of one grey bird.

5

Catbird? Could be. But phantombird for sure
Because no headline names, no screen projects it,
No commentator puts it in the picture.

And you? Are you accounted for, a fixture
Statistically, verifiably human,
New England Francis of the chickadees?

Our zooman, say, our natureman, thick with trees?
Who owns, distributes, packages what you do?
Who's your psychologist? Who's got you taped?

You rape no moon, you rocket-pock no planet.
You celebrate the chickweed's tiny stars.
You planted junipers. You let them grow.

You planted herbs. You let each one distil
From common earth an irresolvable savour.
You tap the maples, and we sipped their sap,

Watery, faintly sweet. But ichor, pure.
Sipped elderflower wine, unlicensed liquor,
Untaxed. The luxury, the arrant cheek

Of loving pure things, choosing to be poor,

6

Always beginners, learners of
Languages we shall never speak
Though listening we are used
By them, and they speak to us
Until our own words crumble
To chickenfeed, birdfeed —

                        Your stillness
In face of their twitter and cheep,
Their flutter and hop, their clinging
To bud and twig upside down,
Their flurry, not to be held,
That touched you, leapt from your hand,

7

Receded. But straight and clean
The sunshine falls, and the shadows
Take their time to turn.

The strangeness hurts, an old wound.
The strangeness burns, but the flame's
Lightness and brightness are new,

Always, day after day,
As it feeds on winds, on wood,
Feeds on words, flesh.

Cat

Unfussy lodger, she knows what she wants and gets it:
Food, cushions, fires, the run of the garden.
I, her night porter in the small hours,
Don't bother to grumble, grimly let her in.
To that coldness she purrs assent,
Eats her fill and outwits me,
Plays hide and seek in the dark house.

Only at times, by chance meeting the gaze
Of her amber eyes that can rest on me
As on a beech-bole, on bracken or meadow-grass,
I'm moved to celebrate the years between us,
The farness and the nearness:
My fingers graze her head.
To that fondness she purrs assent.

Cat, Aging

Her years measure mine.
So finely set in her ways,
She divines, she sniffs out
Every change in the house,
In the weather, and marks it for me
Though with a flick of an ear
Only, a twitch of her tail.
She foretells convolutions,
Departure, thunderstorm,
By not being there — hiding
Behind the heater. At times
She will play yet, kittenish,
Or hunt; but then gathers
All movement, vanity
Into her great stillness
That contains the whole of herself
And more, of her kind. When she stays there,
Dies, it is me she'll prove mortal.

172

Cat, Dying

To be silent, sparing of sound,
Was her way; to be still,
Sparing of movement
Save to leap and land
With precision, even when old,
Where she must, on the stove
Or window-sill, on her prey;
Silent, save to express
Satisfaction by purring,
Hunger by gentle mewing,
Care, long ago,
When she called her kittens,
By low tones;
Day after day, for hours on end,
She would share a stillness with me
On my writing table or desk.
Rarely, before she was older than old,
Failing, did a pain draw
Cries from her in a voice not hers
But pain's voice, a howling;
And soon, again and again
She would recompose
Her silence, restored to herself.

Little silence or stillness
Could accrue to her, then,
After the last spasms;
Mouth and eyes wide-open
With the strain of her dying,
With the pain of it:
Cold at last, rigid,
From her sure centre
Hardly she'd shifted.

When, as I buried her
In the quiet marsh, at evening,
The spade struck stone,
It was the harsh noise that jarred,
Not the lean body
Landing, where it must,
Softly, on black soil.

Dowland

"Pleasant are the tears which music weeps"
And durable, black crystal, each drop keeps
When eyes are dry a glimmer of deep light,
But melting, mixed with wine,
Could move the great to offer gold for brine.
Miraculous exchange!
Until that trade grew strange,
Mere dearth of common bread,
True tears, true absence drained the fountainhead,
Put out in utter night
The glimmer, lost to their eyes, lost to mine.
And then I knew what trade
I'd practised unbeknown:
Of blood not ink was my black music made,
Feigned grief to them so sweet because my own
Transmuted nolens volens
By cruel mastery's menial, semper dolens.
But tearless I depart,
Glad that my lute melts no time-serving heart
And deep in crystal glows dark Dowland's art.

The Cello .

In Memoriam R.H. 1884-1940

Coffined, draped in black
For years it lay
On top of the white wardrobe
And lying sleepless
In that room
Never I heard
The feathery sonata
Dust must have hummed
On the strings left taut
When his fingers tautened
And became dust,
Deaf and dumb beneath
Black boards, black cloth
Beethoven died in his death.

Many removals have brought me
Closer to where he lay,
Faint music from upstairs
Growing fainter, his house
Drifting away into stillness
And all the voices fading.
Now as I hear
Beethoven re-delivered
By tremulous fingers not his
From another cello's womb
It is dust I breathe,
It is dust that trills:
White feathers whirl
In a black room.

Envoi

Goodbye, words.
I never liked you,
Liking things and places, and
Liking people best when their mouths are shut.

Go out and lose yourselves in a jabbering world,
Be less than nothing, a vacuum
Of which words will beware
Lest by suction, your only assertion, you pull them in.

For that I like you, words.
Self-destroyed, self-dissolved
You grow true.
To what? You tell me, words.

Run, and I'll follow,
Never to catch you up.
Turn back, and I'll run.
So goodbye.

V

Observations
Ironies
Unpleasantries

Life and Art I

For Denis Lowson

"A cell," I reply when visitors remark
On the small high windows of the room I work in,
A room without a view. 'Exactly what I need,
Daylight enough — no more — to push a pen by,
And no distractions. Even the two great elms
With their congregations, race riots and social conflicts,
Endless commotion of squirrels, jackdaws and owls
Not to be seen, and only seldom heard.'

You dropped in one morning and sketched the garden,
All blue and black with the bulk and shade of those elms.
At once I longed to possess it. (The garden, the sketch?)
And above my desk I pinned up the silence extracted
From the endless commotion of squirrels, jackdaws and owls.
My garden hangs on the wall — and no distractions.

Life and Art II

Because I was writing my poem on sticklebacks —
Day in, day out, again and again
Till I scrapped it, tore up all the drafts —
I forgot to feed them. Mere babies, they gobbled up
Every unarmoured, toothless and spikeless creature
Left alive in the tank,
(Tinier still they'd picked off
The fry of fishes potentially four times their size)
To the last mouthful charged and bit one another
Then weakened and died.

I loved them, of course,
(Nil inhumani etc. — as long as it's nature:
Frogs collide with toads in my creepery garden)
Their fins always aquiver,
Their mottled mackerel sheen,
How they shot, torpedoes in search of ships —

179

And was full of remorse.
I'd been waiting to see the males
Flush carmine, magnesium blue in the breeding season,
Bravely defend their nests.

Yet my conscience took comfort, too, at the thought:
One love poem less.

Life and Art III

(Lilium 'myriophyllum var.superbum' — or 'sulphureum')

1

Somewhere in Burma, with no special effort
And ignorant of its name, this lily grew,
Making sure of survival three times over
Like other delicate kinds: by simple seed
(Requiring fertilization), stem bulbil and bulb scale —
The last to insure that even the parent's decay
Should be potent for propagation; and still grows there
If the same graeco-latinizing species
That classified the lily and gave itself
The name of homo sapiens has left intact
This lily's habitat, somewhere in Burma.

2

Twenty-odd years ago a colleague gave me
A seed — or was it a bulbil?
Intrigued by the name, by the rarity,
And expecting a flower all sulphur-yellow,
I potted the thing, raised a seedling,
Saw it die down, reappear,
Watered, fed it, repotted it,
Moved it from house to house, from county to county,
Took bulbils again and again
From stems too slender to flower,
Potted new seedlings year after year,

Saw them die down, reappear,
Planted some out, kept others behind glass,
Tried this and that, and waited and waited and waited;

3

Hardly expectant by now; out of a habit of hope,
Of tending the potentiality of a flower
All sulphur-yellow, superb, exotic.

To think of it was to wonder
Whether over the years
I hadn't lost it, the nucleus,
Muddled it up with more common sorts,
Tigrinum, *auratum* or what do you call it,
That had come and gone, duly flowered and seeded
Or failed, as lilies will;
Left it behind perhaps in a place forgotten about
Or let it rot in some pot or other.

4

But here it is at last, long art's reward,
Two plants, not one, come to maturity
In adverse conditions, a long way from Burma,
Late in the season, too, taking their time.
And long the buds were, strangely blotched with green
And pink — not sulphur-yellow at all,
Until they opened. The yellow was deep inside
The long white petals, darker, richer than sulphur,
Deeper than in *regale*; the fragrance heavier still
Than *regale's*, with a stronger sort of vanilla
Blended than in *regale* with *candidum's* pure honey.

5

And now? I have lost a habit
Of hope; and must find another
Seed, bulbil, scale, root
That will take as long or longer

To fulfil itself, in adverse conditions;
As much work, as much bother,
Enough to last out my life, outlast it.

As for that lily, superb, exotic,
Though not sulphur-yellow at all,
To be candid, it's *candidum* I prefer,
The simple cottage lily that grows in these parts
With no special effort, ignorant of its name.

An Inspiration

This morning I thought that perhaps
Only the unpublished poem preserves its worth,
That to publish it is to cast it
Into a rubbish dump to decompose
Together with last week's murders and Football Pools,
Stock prices, social occasions and statements of policy.
The quirk convinced me. Quickly I typed it out
And to a well-known weekly despatched these lines.

Words

"A writer you call yourself? And sit there tongue-tied
While others talk about books?
Jolted, answer in monosyllables, non-committal at that.
Are you shy, then, or sly? Superior or plain dim-witted?
Do we bore you, or aren't you there?"

"A bit of all these. But words are the root of the trouble.
Because I can't speak — what I can't speak — I write.
Words? Yes, words. I can't do without them.
But I hate them as lovers hate them
When it's time for bodies to speak;
As an acrobat would,
Asked to tell how he leaps, why he leaps, when he's leaping.

A curious trade, I admit:
Turning a thing into words so that words will render the thing;
Setting a movement to words so that words will render the
    movement.
But words about words about things? I can do without them.
Look: the arc-lamp's game with the plane-tree's windblown
    branches.
Listen: an owl. And those voices — closing time down the
    street.
And smell: the coffee boiled over two minutes ago."

Progress

Take rhetoric and wring its neck.
Ditto, with anti-rhetoric.
Then, poet, all temptation gone
To fake or posture, wring your own.

Poor Performance

Why is your tone so low, so low,
Why is your tone so thin? —
Because I'm playing solo, solo
On a plastic violin.

Crise de Foie

"As for serving, our livers will do that for us."
Adam, Head Waiter at the *Wild Isle*

And did they? In their lifetime pickled,
Living it up? When revolution came,
Non serviam on every manjack's bib,
Lords of your kidney drew long faces
And, galled by common fare, lost heart.
A Finnish soup, Sibelius
Too soon ran out. No other course remained.
The white-gloved Maître, the finnicky Chef
Mopped the last plates and scrubbed the floor.

In Philistia

Thoughts after a public reading of new verse

'To affirm the affirmative'. Yes.
With a lean or a fat smirk
To confirm: that's how we are, human.
Not to shirk nappies,
Knowingly to acknowledge
I know what you know:
That people may laugh or vomit
In face of their dead,
Lovers may bore each other,
The bomb is the bomb.

Tedious economy:
Those pennies they drop in our hats
We spin or jingle for them,
They thank us for showing them pennies.

Not sapiens, though, but quaerens
(Excuse the presumption of Latin)
They walk when we are not looking,
We walk when oblivious of them.

184

Vehicles I

But you preferred my "one" and "he" and "we"?
My reticence? Humility? Liked me more
When wrapped in myth and mask and metaphor
I kept my beasts heraldic, men heroic,
Rhythm and stanza tidy, bearing stoic?
Before, a blabber, I loosed "the odious me"?

Humble? I cared for it, I made a fuss
Of that indifferent, second-hand machine,
(It looked as good as new) for ever busy
Maintaining, patching up my poor tin lizzy,
So anxious that to keep the panels clean
And spare the engine I would go by bus.

And now? I like it more and less
All scraped and dented, in a mess
My boneshaker that still keeps going.
It's past re-chroming now, re-spraying,
Past washing too. And so I let
The garage, park it in the street.
I cannot sell it, cannot lose it,
Can neither spoil it nor misuse it
Though far I drive it, drive it hard,
Knowing that in the breaker's yard
Something will last, perhaps to move
What singular and plural cove —
But not the paintwork, not the chrome:
No car of mine will drive me home.

Vehicles II

Every time I use the first person singular in a poem
It calls to mind that more than three quarters of the people on
    earth
Can no more afford an ego than they can a Cadillac,
Let alone a singular person. If one of them says 'I'
He or she means the need that makes a baby cry;
And food isn't singular. As for the pampered few
The luxury and autonomy of their egos can be such
As to bore them. In that plight they'll resort
To drugs or the forms of meditation practised
Where 'I' permutes from 'anyone' to 'no one'; and may even toy
With the disciplines of self-abnegation, of poverty.
That calls to mind all these Yogis in Cadillacs.

Telephone Poem

Halloh.
                    Who's that?

Words.
                    Who's Words?

Whose words? Anyone's.
Heard by me, recorded,
Heard by you, overheard,
Their person is the third.
                    Come off it. Say who you are.

Words, near and far,
Everyday, strange
In their want of wanting...
                    Exchange?
                    Anonymous call. Can you trace it?
You made it. Computers can't place it,
Decode it. Your listening can,
On the loose, free-range.
Caller, to cancel that call,
Words meant for no one, all,
Dial a silence. Or face it.

Letter

I looked at it, I stared
At the one-word message:
SUCCESS!
Whose could it be?
And as I stared
The one worm at the beginning,
The two worms at the end
Wriggled away.
The stake drove down —
Into what heart, what centre?

Eros

Big shot? Bad shot. Bungler.
With a fine arrowhead pierces
The wrong breast,
Lets a blunt one
Bounce off the right.
Arrested. For ever a kid.

Gallant to the End

Knotting his favourite necktie, a rope,
The lifeline of one whose insanity
Is not to take dope, not to hope,
He's reminded: who to himself will not lie
Will lie with no one.
Also: accursed are those
Who have not vanity.
Zombie knows.

If you leave me, the lover's gambit had run,
I shall die.
Moved by the compliment,
She had wept — and walked out.
Egregiously, though, he had meant
Every word of it. That's what the joke is about.

One Flesh

When Miranda left George
After fourteen years of marriage
To take a lover, discard
Dustpan and pinafore,
Refurbish if she could
The toys of her girlhood,
He felt his left leg freeze,
Hobbled about, still hopeful,
But gasped with the dragging, collapsed.
Amputation was called for.
Above the knee.
                     The paralysis
Was arrested. The pain
Moved to where he was not.
Now he hopped as fast with his crutches
As ever he'd walked before limping.
He was about to try on
The prosthetic limb just ready
When Miranda telephoned:
"Darling, I'm coming home.
It was all a mistake, you see...
Unexpected? Well, yes, like all good things...
But you did say you wanted me back."

Bestial

Seeing a lone urban frog clamped to a panicking goldfish,
A caged monkey masturbate, a cow mount a cow
Or one male dog another,
Zombie preaches:
Dear animals, what are you coming to?
Are you ascending the evolutionary scale
Too fast? Is domestication making you
Human?
Bless you, animals, but beware;
Or soon you'll be coupling the whole year round
With no time for meditation —
Full-time lovers in need of psychiatrists.

Mal d'Autrui

She comes, my headache, my bellyache,
My toothache to torment me.
With moist, with mad eyes
That mean no harm, so full
Of her luxurious grieving
Their nature is not to see —
Geysers of other-pain
In whose hot vapours I gasp,
They scald me with their gushing
Till, cold, I shrink away.

Unfeeling? Murderous now
With pity that she disdained
Who swore to kill herself
And punish the world for not caring,
I care too much to be cruel,
Too little now to implore:
My headache, bellyache, toothache,
Worse than all these, outside me,
Despair of dentist and doctor,
Forgive me for not being you.

189

Sick Transit

Gloria Mundy, the fashion model,
Hand on hip, steps
From the Paris-London 'plane,
Her luggage this autumn's inanity
Carried with blank poise
From blank face to
Blank face;
From bank to bank.

Solidarity

There's honour among thieves, both in and out of prison,
Fellowship even, in the teeth of competition,
And sorority among whores — though mainly off-duty,
On sea-side vacations, or after the ruin of beauty —
But strongest and strangest of all is the solidarity
Of respectable men in respectable company.
Would it be drink that does it? Dissolving differences,
Discrete achievements and individual purities?
No, they feel it when sober, not only at parties and luncheons,
But in boardrooms, common rooms, barracks, or charging
     with truncheons.
It comes over them suddenly — not a warm, not a vernal
     breath,
Yet kindling warmth in cold hearts — the bad conscience of
     death,
Communist at the frontier bound in time to break through,
But, teacher of love among convicts, Christian too.

Homo Sum: Humani Nihil etc.

For H.M.E.

Too true. Don't say it. Don't.
Trujillo. Hero and owner of a nation,
Honoured and served by men, himself a man,
Upheld, abetted by the lords of commerce,
Dealers in sugar, dealers in carrion —
All men. What else? And the carrion also human.

To be grass, to be cud for cows. Not to know
The taste of meat or the taste of sugar,
To rise again from mud and be green,
Eat mud, eat carrion, but not with a human mouth.

Observer

The newspaper in my hands
Reports a four-sided battle
In the streets of a town
I shall never see.
What I see, what I read
Will depend on this war,
The sum and ratio of men
Maimed or killed on each side.

The newspaper in my hands
Omits to count the losses
On a fifth side — the people.
Yet the winner, if any, will count
The people, if any, left over
Because with no people to rule
The winners would not be the winners,
The war itself would not count.

The newspaper in my hands
Will serve to light a fire,
Yesterday's casualties burn
On my grate tomorrow
Or perhaps with dead leaves in the garden;
Tomorrow's newspaper bring me
Headlines that cancel out
Yesterday's interim score.

The newspaper in my hands
Begins to smoulder, to stink
As I read the day's gossip
About business and fashion,
Parties and mergers and
This gossip-monger's views
On a news handout on
A book on a fashion-pimp.

The newspaper in my hands
Begins to rot my hands.
I drop the newspaper, stare:
From my right forefinger
Something obtrudes. I pinch it
And pull out a worm, then another.

I look at my left hand:
Hollowed out, a black stump.
Amid all those woodlice
Scurrying there I spot
A big slug. With a matchstick held
Between worm-eaten fingers
I spear the slug, remove it.
And nothing hurts. Nothing.

Two Photographs

1
At an outdoor table of the Café Heck
In the Munich Hofgarten
Six gentlemen in suits
And stiff white collars
Are sitting over coffee,
Earnestly talking.
The one with a half-moustache
Wears a trilby hat.
The others have hung up theirs,
With their overcoats, on hooks
Clamped to a tree.
The season looks like spring.
The year could be '26.

On a hook otherwise bare
Hangs a dogwhip.

No dog appears in the picture —

An ordinary scene.
Of all the clients
At adjoining tables
None bothers to stare.

2
The year is '33.
The gentleman in a trilby
Is about to board a train.
Behind him stand
Four men in black uniforms.
'For his personal protection'
The Chancellor of the Reich
Carries a dogwhip.

No dog appears in the picture.

Footnote on a Neglected Writer

For nearly two decades, under the bourgeois régime,
N lived in poverty and, for the privileged few,
A Marxist critic objected, published the stories and poems
Which O, the same critic, called workmanlike, though
    demanding.
N took the stricture to heart; even before the Coup
Vowed he would write for the people; did, and became
Famous, powerful, rich, one of the few now privileged
To take part in the drafting of programmes, the fixing of
    cultural norms.
Yet his output, if anything, grew, because productivity
Must be kept up in all fields; till O, who had barely survived
The latest purge, abused the access allowed him
To the periodical Z, by hinting that N's latest novel
In praise of factory workers was convincing neither in detail
Nor in conception. O was given the choice
Between eating his words and learning by first-hand
    experience
What manual labour is like. Not in the best of health,
He cheerfully chose the latter.
                      N's conveyance to O
Of his grief and shock proved sincere. Punctilious as ever
At congresses, meetings, he'd rise from a sleepless night
Blankly to face the blank paper, 'workmanlike', 'workmanlike',
'Workmanlike' hammered into his consciousness, nail after
    nail.

The Soul of Man under Capitalism

Looks for its body among
The skyscrapers, tenement blocks
Where a white man's unwise to walk.
At the thought of revolution
Sends kites, balloons into air opaque
With excremental vapours of produce
And sees them vanish, glad
That where they've gone they'll be free.
Meanwhile it feeds refrigerators
With bags of lobster tails, whole sides of prime beef,
Homogenized milk by the gallon; and, hailed by Donuts,
By Steak or Chicken Dinner it glides
Down Main Street emptily, starving
For the smell of newly baked bread.

Report on a Supermarket

1

First of all, the site:
Nowhere, I said, put it nowhere,
Right out of town — some town! —
Near the motel, if you like, near the filling station,
But away from houses, all houses.
You wouldn't listen. And now
People drive in for a pack or two
Of cigarettes and — would you believe it? —
Walk in and buy what they want.
Walk — do you get me? — on their own legs,
And buy what *they* want, in dribbles.
That's what comes of the site — retrogression.
I warn you: soon they'll be asking
For fresh food, bread from small bakeries,
Milk unhomogenized, unrefrigerated,
Local fruit and vegetables and fish,
All the small-time produce that once gave us trouble.

2

Next, there are losses, bad losses.
Take eggs: billions of them each year
Crack, a write-off. You needn't tell me
The scientists are working on that —
Tougher shells, to be guaranteed
By diet or injections. But we can't wait.
Injection, that's it: have the whole goddamn egg
Injected into plastic shells, there's your answer.
Then invent a cracking machine, and the makers
Will subsidize the whole process for you.
Natural eggs, in any case,
Are too cheap, not worth marketing.
Plastic shells will cost more.

3

Last, but worst, the housewives —
Retrogressive, I tell you, and unreliable,
Poor material, even the regulars
Who shop by the week, for the icebox —
Like the one ten days ago, an old customer,
Not a red — we can smell them — not an egghead,
Complained that her Florida oranges,
That line with the colour added, our best line,
Were rotten and poisoned a dinner guest
Dear to her, and her husband's career.
Under pressure the woman confessed
That she'd set the table that morning
Taken the oranges from where they belong
And left them all day in a fruit bowl.
"Creative arrangement", she kept on protesting;
"Negligence, madam, waste", I corrected her,
Giving her all the statistics, the handouts.
She tore them up and never came back.

4

Worst, did I say? Well, there's worse to come.
Just picture a model customer,
Middle-aged, no worries at all,
Three grown-up children at Ivy League schools,
Three automobiles — comes in a Cadillac,
Begins her round, as usual, at the meat counter
But goes green in the face and starts hollering:
"Get me out of here! Get me out of this morgue!
Never again! I vow that I'll organize
A nation-wide hunger strike, or live on wild berries!"
What could I do but smile and escort her out?

5

Now, that kind of thing has happened before.
Bad for prestige? You're kidding.
Here's my prescription: have special trolleys made
For emergency cases like that one, strap them down,
Force-feed them with all they need,
Proteins, carbohydrates, vitamins, the lot,
From a mixer-feeder I can design,
Injecting a full week's provisions.
Their families? OK, they're another problem,
But the system's prestige would rocket sky-high.
For legal reasons the service could function gratis,
With detergents thrown in, toilet rolls and the rest.
Later a minimal charge would be best
Till the service is recognized, and catches on.
Life-Saver, we'd call it, and gain live advertisements.
If the demand became too great
We need only raise the price
And establish a revolutionary technique,
A new norm in our free-world economy.
Patent the process, that's my advice,
And you'll never look back.

An Error

"U.S. Offers Condolence and Aid to Vietnamese Bombed in Error"
New York Times, 29 September 1966

1

There is rejoicing at Hombe:
Only thirty-five persons died,
Only seventeen were injured
As compared with a hundred and sixteen thatch and wattle
    homes destroyed.
This means that most of the people
Must have been out of the hamlet
When the Marine 'plane pilots
Made their little mistake,
Bombing not reds but allies,
Members of the militia force, their wives and children.

2

There is rejoicing at Hombe:
Each dead person's next of kin
Has already received
The standard condolence payment,
Four thousand piastres or about thirty-four dollars,
And lesser amounts
Went to the wounded, depending
Upon the extent of their injuries.
Furthermore, survivors
Are expected to sue the United States
For additional compensation —
A standard procedure, virtually,
In such circumstances,
Circumstances virtually standard by now.

3

There is rejoicing at Hombe:
Never before have the villagers
Made a profit out of the death
Of a nearest relative. Never
Has the richest of them supposed
That a life could be worth so much money
Or that governments could be sued
For what, after all, must happen sooner or later.

4

There is rejoicing at Hombe,
Mingled with dissatisfaction:
Bomb us again, they beg,
Our protectors, our liberators,
We still have people to spare
But not enough rice to feed them,
Now that the fields are churned up.
Let the survivors be few,
So that cousins and uncles and nieces
May earn them wealth more like yours
Whose corpses in funeral parlours
Lie radiant, as good as alive,
Or frozen await resurrection.
Let them leave the site, then, for ever,
And the ghosts of kin they had loved.
Blast Hombe out of your maps and our minds.

After a War

The outcome? Conflicting rumours
As to what faction murdered
The one man who, had he survived,
Might have ruled us without corruption.
Not that it matters now:
We're busy collecting the dead,

Counting them, hard though it is
To be sure what side they were on.
What's left of their bodies and faces
Tells of no need but for burial,
And mutilation was practised
By Right, Left and Centre alike.
As for the children and women
Who knows what they wanted
Apart from the usual things?
Food is scarce now, and men are scarce,
Whole villages burnt to the ground,
New cities in disrepair.

The war is over. Somebody must have won.
Somebody will have won, when peace is declared.

Little Cosmology

In the beginning was business. But the facts are obscure
Because no accounts were kept and even the Founder's person
Is veiled in mystery. All we know is the rules
Passed on to the management by one of such absolute power,
So revered and so rarely seen that even to speak his name
Was a deadly offence. And who can deny that a residue
Of that primal awe still adheres to the policy-making
Heads of corporations, whatever the system and ownership?
Our six-day week (where not yet reduced to five)
Goes back to that mythical phase and the rules laid down
By the Father of Commerce. Likewise from earliest records
We learn how this Earth with its minerals, flora and fauna
And finally Man, was created — needless to say
As material for business, which was in the beginning,
Though we also read of the Word (or Logos), the medium
Which more than other human attributes, even including
Our manual skill and inventiveness, furthered the progress
Of business from primitive barter to modern finance.
For words and numbers permitted the gradual transition
From chattel to coin and lastly paper economies.

This is called evolution: the origin of species =
('A particular sort of coin or money. Coinage, coin,
Money bullion. Metal used for coinage.' Oxford English
        Dictionary)
Is the key to history proper. And words mark the
        turning-points,
As when somebody, doubtless a man of genius,
Coined this figure of speech, 'The Shop of State',
Showing sudden total awareness of that which distinguishes
Our highly developed nation states from all that had gone
        before,
Or when Napoleon called England 'a nation of shopkeepers',
A description at that time construed as less than a
        compliment,
Although it was more, a prophecy based on the recognition
Of how the Industrial Revolution had changed the structure
Of one great nation, as later it must every other's
Regardless of whether its products and prices and rate of
        investment
Were controlled by cartel, competition or state monopoly.

So much for history. Henceforth we may take it for granted
That the cosmos itself and human life on this planet
With its institutions and enterprises, organization and laws
Has, and was meant to have, only one ultimate end,
The growth and perfection of business, of wealth and of
        power.
It remains to clear up a number of seeming complexities,
Conflicts and contradictions. E.g. a few men and women
Have been heard to grumble like this: "A consumer society?
Haven't people always consumed? And isn't the point about
        ours
That we have to consume whatever is put on the market,
Not what *we* want? A producer society, then,
It ought to be called." Well, apart from the quibble,
That objection condemns the objector as one with no proper
        concern
In the shop of state; a misfit, parasite, drop-out
Whom psycho-ideological tests will invariably prove
To harbour an atavistic, anti-historical, irreligious

Craving for simple 'things' — a form of regression
No civilized order can tolerate, the point about ours
Being that it rests not on 'things' but on tokens
Or symbols — like money, commodities, words.
The very same truth confutes the subversive chatter of those
Who charge our world with 'materialism'. A world in which
     matter
Has ceased to matter — can that be materialistic?
It's the token, the symbol that counts. Which brings us back
To where we began — to the mystery.
Our shopkeepers, up to the hierarchies
Of Presidents, Chairmen, Prime Managers, may forget
What ancient flame they are guardians of, what holy office
     they serve,
What authority, vested in them, they administer.
Yet, rightly, we praise and adore them and fear their might.
So be it, then; as it was in the beginning
And ever shall be, except for improvements,
Inevitable adjustments, fluctuations in currency values.

Credo

Some argue that the universe is expanding.
We know it's expendable.
Others argue that the universe is contracting.
We know it's contracted for.
Put a parking lot on Mars
And folks will go there, forget about breathing.
Put a supermarket on Venus
And it's ripe for development.
Let the universe shrink or bust:
Civilization — and that means us —
Will keep moving from deal to deal.

Big Deal

The smartest, greatest and most American
Of all those great Presidents
Had this brainwave: a package deal.
Why not simplify, putting the whole great country
From Maine to California, Alaska to Florida,
On the market. Right. Put it up for sale.
Not only her natural and unnatural resources,
Grand Canyon, Pentagon, Howard Johnson, Niagara Falls
And the rest, but the know-how and ethos,
The secret of making folks want what they do not need.

Strange, though the moon was thrown in,
And the means of getting there, it was not
That nobody could afford it —
Long-term credit was offered,
With no down-payment at all —
But that nobody wanted to buy.

Conversion

A Letter

I was watching commercials, as usual, just at the time
When the News interrupts them. There was this war,
Kept going, they said, to maintain the balance of power —
A distraction from laxatives. Then came next year's models,
Automobiles, and that was normal, but they were pushed
    out
By a long speech — the ex-Vice-President's. He seemed to
    be saying
That a deal was made: If he refrained from contesting
One little charge the law court would exempt him
Both from further charges and from the full penalty
For that one. What wasn't clear was whether or not
He had done the thing he was charged with. However,
His overall innocence was as convincing as
The justice of his conviction, considering that he had chosen

Not to deny his guilt — under pressure from people unnamed
Even bigger than he had been when he had the power
To apply such pressure. Moreover he sacrificed
His career so that others could go on applying
This kind of pressure and justice. If that wasn't big
Of him, the ex-Vice-President, what is or ever has been
As long as deals have been made? So my overall response
To his protestation of overall innocence was total.
He deserves a statue, believe me, nearly as big
As the Statue of Liberty. Because next to liberty —
The liberty to make deals if you're big enough,
Big as the ex-Vice-President or the people unnamed
Who're bigger even than he was before they made the deal
That gave him the chance to sacrifice his career —
Nothing is dearer to us these days or more in demand
Than innocence. And no wonder. It works far better than
    laxatives.
How could we function without it? I mean, how could we
Buy and sell all there is to be bought and sold
If innocence didn't make us a hundred percent sure
That buying and selling are innocent? Thanks to the speech,
    then,
I can enjoy commercials *and* be quite sold on the News.

Belated Prologue

to an impromptu address on 'Freedom' at a
Liberal Arts College

Freely, my captive listeners, question or interrupt
The impostor imposed upon you. For poets, I freely admit,
Are not thinkers but feelers. (Note, if you like, the
    sweepingness
Of that claim; all the possible meanings of 'feelers';
The allusion to Pound on 'antennae'. You look puzzled
    already.
Please don't make me explain, or the poet's freedom is lost.)
Crackers? That's right. A great many poets are crackers,
Compulsively cracking words as though they were nuts,

204

Words like 'Freedom'. What for? Out of an urge to discover
Multiple meat in the maggoty pulp of black walnuts,
The hard shells of hickory — a notorious nuttiness
Hardly relished by guardians of any Republic,
From Plato's to Stalin's or Nixon's, although in the last
The very freedom that brings me here, the freedom to say
And write what I feel, allows you to yawn
Instead of denouncing or lynching me; and will make you
    applaud
Whatever I say, before you forget all about it...

Pleasure Island

(South Carolina)

Beyond the cottonfields, the swamps, the moss-hung trees
Two bridges now grant easy access to the island
Initiates call Paradise. The serpent too they'll find
Who look for it on nature trails, and alligator,
But never since developers transformed the plots
Of black subsistence farmers and the virgin jungle
Into exquisite residences, landscaped, blended
With palm and shrub, has either animal presumed
To intrude upon that peace or taint that innocence,
Molesting the elect. A harbour was constructed
For yachts, and cabin cruisers of the gamefish anglers
Not out for vulgar food but only to kill time,
Once dearly bought by others, with competitive thrills,
And in their goodness Eden's architects provide
Not only watchers at the gate but harbourside guards
To warn, or to repulse with truncheon and revolver
Poor sinners who might threaten the terrain reserved
For sportsmen, property owners, bona fide guests
Of restaurant, inn, motel. And plan still more. Quite lately
A new amenity, an English pub, was opened,
Adding the tumbledown quaintness of its old barn style
To relics like the heaps of oyster shells that mark
An Indian banqueting site. For clients who prefer
History nearer home, two graveyards, white and black,

In woodland clearings most conveniently recall
What brief and cruel lives masters and servants led
On the same island once, before the sole commandment
'Thou shalt enjoy thyself, thou shalt relax and spend'
Founded its golden age. The wise will pause to look,
Pity their luckless peer whose family mausoleum
Was robbed and left a ruin by soldiers from the Fort,
But will not linger there, far less before tin roofs —
Crude as the children's gravestones — visible on shacks
Not yet incorporated into Paradise
By demolition. Fortified they will return
To beach or golf course, bicycle, horse, beach buggy,
Whichever fits their years, their constitution best,
And, though by working for it, earn an appetite.

Newspaper Story

(Santa Barbara News Press, 16 February 1973)

1

In Hartford City, Indiana,
Lived a factory worker, Gary,
Patriotic enough to invest
What little cash he could spare
In US Savings Bonds.
His reward came in the shape
Of a flag. But not rich enough
To own a house, an apartment
Or a flagpole on which to hang it,
Gary pinned up the flag
In his minibus as a curtain.

2

When Gary was arrested
For desecrating the flag
His hair was noted to be

Of un-American length;
And the minibus, too, his home,
Was not of American make.

3

Just when the Vietnam heroes
Were due for repatriation
Gary was sentenced to bear
Old Glory for three hours
Outside the City Hall.
While police guards stood by
He was watched by a mixed crowd
Of longhairs, Boy Scouts
And American Legionnaires
In full regalia. The word
'Commie' was shouted repeatedly.

4

Gary might have been fined.
But the judge, a patriot too,
Thought public penance more apt.
"The intent was embarrassment,"
He commented later. "A fine
Wouldn't reach that man."

5

"What could I do?" asked Gary.
"I ain't got 1000 dollars.
It wasn't much of a choice.
Either look like an idiot,
Slapped in the stocks, jeered at
As a communist or something,
Or else let my wife and kids
Go hungry."

6

            Strange, in the end
Everyone seemed to weaken.
Gary after one hour
Withdrew to the courtroom, to finish
His penance beneath a plaque
Bearing the pledge of allegiance,
And so made the penance private —
Not, to be sure, because
Of the biting winter winds.
The publicity hurt his credit,
His father's, too, and his wife's.
Indeed he demanded review
Of his case in a Circuit Court.

The judge said: "Being a veteran,
Proud of my country and flag,
I'd probably do it again."

Probably? There was the chink
Where the rot of treason sets in.
That judge was eating crow.

The Truths

The trouble is, they belong to no party, no union, no club
And never go in for politics —
At least not since one of them, P.B. Truth, Independent,
Got three votes and lost his deposit.

The successful candidate, a progressive Conservative,
Promised a boom in agriculture, a free hand for builders,
More respect for parkland, green belts and old villages,
A speeding up of industrial development;
Fewer cars on the roads, a reduction of public expenditure
On railways, buses and any form of transport
Unable to prove its worth in a free economy;
Tax reliefs for certified lepers and destitute octogenarians
And the setting up of a standing committee
Responsible for appointing experts
Who would enquire into the possibilities
Of how obsolete nuclear rockets
Might be sold to potential enemies
In the interest of peace and scientific advancement,
Or otherwise exploited for the nation's prosperity.

The family can't be extinct. Every now and then
A short letter appears in *The Times*
Signed by one or the other Truth,
But without an address.
The trouble is, they can't be bothered to shout,
To cajole, or even to argue at length,
Drawing on helpful statistics.
To put it bluntly, the Truths are a lazy lot,
Not indifferent perhaps, but behaving as though they were,
Always expecting others to run after *them*.
No wonder they don't ever count.

Legal Problem

A day of the life of a man or woman —
What is it worth, in hard figures?

London Transport once worked it out:
Those who travel on trains with no proper ticket or warrant
(With intent to avoid payment)
Upon a second or subsequent offence
Are liable to a fine of twenty-five pounds
Or three months in prison.

A day of the life of a man or woman
Is worth five shillings five pence and roughly three farthings
(Or twenty-seven new pence and a half, not allowing for
    inflation)
That is, a day of the life of a man or woman
Unable to pay a fine of twenty-five pounds.

Irrefutable though it is, the solution
Leaves a loose end or two:
Granted a day of a poor man's, poor woman's life
Is worth twenty-seven new pence and a half, not allowing for
    inflation,
What of the man or woman so poor, so deprived
That freedom is worth less than nothing to him or to her?
How can she or he be punished, unable to pay the fine?
How persuaded to waive her claim, his claim to a cell?

And, granted the question will always remain hypothetical:
A day of a rich man's, rich woman's life
Out of prison, what is it worth?

Squares

A misnomer, really. With a few exceptions —
The very dumpy and squat — we're rectangular.
Why? Because of our frames, of course:
Invisible frames that expand as we grow.
At times they crack. Then we grow bigger than you.
And even within the frames there's room for big bodies.

The drawbacks? They're obvious. When two of us meet
We rub edges. Round holes give us trouble —
At first, till the frames have ceased to collide.
Most of us, most of the time, are aware of our corners.
That restricts our freedom. We're obsessed with portraits:
Ancestors, heroes, idols, or plain stuffed shirts.

Rectangles rule our lives: when we write poems
They come out as rectangles (not like yours
That zigzag or snake or frogleap all over the place).
When we dabble in action painting
The frame, foreknown, inhibits our movements.
Coffins too are designed for our frames.

As for you, the smaller of us (the majority)
Hate or envy your guts and your frameless ease;
Frightened, at heart; worried about ourselves:
There's a glut of portraits. The junk yards are full of them,
As the graveyards of coffins, the school anthologies
Of neat rectangular stanzas. What will become of ours?

What will become of you, I wonder. You also proliferate,
Sprawling, slouching, organically squelching and gushing.
Already you look to the East: for flexible frames
That may stiffen with use, if not shrink.
Look out when corners form. Or all those little old rectangles
Will be gaping and whispering: Did you see that? A square!

Lines Discovered in a London Dustbin

North Kensington

Hung up on true love and all that jazz
I looked for a woman among
the miniskirts miniminds maxipresumptions
and found combinations of
sex and pot pot and drink drink and sex
mixed and offered like cocktails
with male and female organs
now here now there so that in the end I wondered
to whom they belonged.
My conclusion was: no one.
Thrill computers about as predictable
as those moon mites packed into capsules
to infest with multiple gadgets
the virginal pale one who long
by remote control had ruled
the lunatic the lover and the poet.
Amplified emptiness deafened me.
I starved in a world full of feedback.

Retrogressive I turned to terrestrial nature
and all that jazz —
O Woods O Fountains Hillocks Dales and Bowrs —
only to read in the papers
that two Belgian microbiologists
had abolished nature, inducing a symbiosis
of plants with bacteria,
laboratory marriages that would lead
to unheard-of mutations
and establish man as the ultimate manipulator
of so-called entelechy, his own included.
May-be, may-be not. There was always the bomb,
another agent of change. But either way it seemed likely
that one day nothing more would remain on this earth
to be botched. And that was enough to make me apologize
to animals plants bacteria
for having taken their names in vain.
I received an answer: excommunication.

There was always the bomb. And protest.
Duly I had protested —
quite lately against the imprisonment
by a right-wing dictatorship
of a left-wing intellectual
whose last public gesture before the event
had been to protest against the protest
occasioned by the imprisonment
by a left-wing dictatorship
of two left-wing intellectuals
who disliked dictatorships.
This made it necessary to protest
that I had protested not in favour of the protest
against the protest but only
against the imprisonment; and that in future
I should feel it incumbent on me to protest
against protests against the protests
of those who protested as I had done
against the imprisonment of protesters.
But the good resolution
proved too much even for bad verse:
blue in the face with impossible contortions
my muse fell dead, strangled by her own arms.
Her last words were a protest: protest and all that jazz...

Well, I could have cashed in on the lady's demise,
rid at last of a troublesome accessory
long outmoded in any case, expensive to keep up,
an extravagance really now that surrogates
are a drug on the market, posters
count more than poems and gossip columns
have replaced immortality. All that was needed
for a new career was to make myself useful
to the dealers in fame fashion fun,
becoming a personality — if only it weren't
for something perverse in me that prefers
to be cold clean unremarkable
dust or ash, which cannot be sold.
In short I'm packing it up, going
underground for good, defecting

to the other side. And promptly too,
before the social planners install
death-wish detectors in every home,
with powers to impose the life penalty
for so much as a day-dream of crossing the border.
I leave no advice no property
and no poems. Only these posthumous lines.

A Fable

"Cats of the world unite
For the great, for the good fight,
For the right of all cats
To live in flats
Or houses if they prefer,"
Cried Growler, the revolutionary cat,
And made quite a stir.

"Fair enough", said the planners,
"We'll do our best
To comply with your request.
But stop waving those banners.
It takes time and negotiation
To push through the legislation
Which in principle we're anxious to enforce."

"Don't give us that",
Hissed Growler, the revolutionary cat.
"We want action now,
Not promises, deeds:
Homes for all colours, all breeds.
Or our anger will take its course.
Can't you see? We're bristling for a row."

Along came Flog,
The counter-revolutionary dog,
And he barked out: "Rights?
We'll show those parasites
Who go their own way.
We'll accommodate that scum
In transit camps, *en route* to Kingdom Come.

We'll get rid of the lot,
Siamese, Persian, what-not.
Dogland for dogs, I say.
Dogs of the nation unite
For the great, for the good fight,
For law and order and might.
Remember: Bite and Obey!"

Bilaterally harassed,
The planners, greatly embarrassed,
Called out the police in force
Who, strictly impartial of course,
With truncheon, boot, horse
Protected the weak from the strong.
Or vice versa? A guess could well prove wrong.

So, for the moment, friend,
The fable has no end,
But in the crush and confusion
Lost sight of its own conclusion,
Which vanished round a bend.
That goes for the moral too —
Not to be found or heard from in that hullabaloo.

How to Beat the Bureaucrats

For Reiner Kunze

You can't hit them: they're paper-thin.
You can't hurt them: the paper is not their own.
Yet fight them we must, we who are peaceable
And feel pain, or all will be paper.

They waste your time. It will cost you
More of your time, all the leisure they've left you.
They drain your energy. It will cost you more,
All the wit, all the zest they have left you.

Yes. Fill in those forms. So minutely
That it's harder for them to sift
The relevant facts from those you have sent as a bonus
Than it was for you to compound the mixture.

Invent complications more abstract even than those
They afflict you with. Further sub-divide
Their sub-divisions. Force them to print new forms,
Open departments, engage new specialists

To meet your case. Overfeed their computers,
Till they spew only pure mathematics, deplete themselves
And close down for mystical meditation
On the infinite fractions of nothing. Meanwhile

Bombard the computers' feeders with more and more paper,
Till from paper and ink a man or woman emerges,
Word is made flesh; and, gasping in piles of paper,
They learn again the first of our needs, to breathe.

Ah, and the file will yield up its leaves to unclassified winds,
Inspectors inspect themselves and promptly submit
Applications in triplicate for their own dismissal,
And the clerk will lie down with the client.

Irish Questions

For Dennis and Julie

I

What can they find here to feed on,
All these Irish corvidae,
The black and the hooded crows,
The rooks, the magpies, the choughs,
Ubiquitous jackdaws, lone ravens,
With the live sheep even so sparse
On Wicklow's bare hills?
Or the sparrow-hawks, where no sparrows chirped?

A great hunger it must be
For them too, though they seem to thrive
On desolation, on emptiness,
Competing with gulls on the coasts,
Competing with nothing
Above the open or covered wounds
The peat-cutters leave;
Above the alien mansions
Abandoned or burnt out,
Alien gardens and parks
Lying vacant behind closed gates
Till the bogs take over again;
Above alien barracks that guarded the landlords once
And did so still when cleared to house
The delinquent offspring of tenants;
Above the little church
Whose roof of stone resisted,
And the monks' fortress, intact,
Slate grave-slab long weathered nameless,
Cross or two still upright,
Ancient trees dropping their branches.

Black against black,
Grey against grey,
Crows glide and land
Under travelling clouds,
Now bedraggled in sudden showers,
Now glossy in sunshine,
Grey, black against green.

II

Your mantic Ireland, Yeats, where is it?
No faeryland I flew to visit,
Not Countess Cathleen, nor Maud Gonne,
No Celtic twilight counted on,
Wanted no blarney, grown too old
Some thirty years since I was told
I'd "ghosted for your ghost". (That too
Was literature, more neat than true.)
Where was it ever, William Yeats,
Save in your loves and in your hates,
Itself a ghost whose invocation
Made you the inventor of a nation?
From Dublin to the Galway shores
I looked for that ghost, and for yours,
Asking myself, can ghosts be banished,
Displaced because their haunts have vanished,
The sites that kept them there have grown
Unrecognizable, unknown?
The granite and the thatch knocked down
For garish bungalows in rows
And ribbon fronts on motorways,
With cattle grazing where they may
On verges, as in Mexico.
Unmourned, unburied, dogs decay
Where travellers' caravans had cluttered
The lay-bys, moved, and left them littered
With a detritus that's world-wide:
New commerce and its underside,
Old poverty, without the pride,
The swagger that was all the rage

218

In your time, processed for the stage.

One asset, though, I saw abound
Up in the sky and on the ground,
From hills to plain, from sea to sea,
Water, a superfluity!
The Shannon's wealth of it alone!
Flooded square miles reflect the sun
On would-be pasture at Athlone,
Fit now for moorhen or for swan.
And where the rapids rush, it vies
With far Niagara now, supplies
The power you had no mind to praise,
Utilitarian energies.

Ah, Coole and Ballylee! Your tower
Looms gaunt, but lonelier, more austere
Now that glum academics tour
The precincts and the winding stair
Whose gyres can lead them anywhere
But to the art you practised there,
Heroics hammered from despair.
And knowingly. On dereliction
You'd founded all your truth and fiction,
Knew even while the stone stood fast
That insubstantial words outlast
The substance they are fed upon.
Your stanzas hold. The house is gone.
Box hedges line the paths that none
Your verses named will walk again.
Names on a tree's bark can be read
By strangers walking there instead,
A canine grave perpetuates
More names, but not your loves and hates.
Black, black, surviving yew-trees mark
The site you cannot haunt, Coole Park,
And on the dark lake's face no white
Of your wild swan's wings would alight.

Elsewhere, in city streets remote
From what you cared about and wrote,
But changed, changed utterly by action
Of internecine creed and faction,
Your frantic Ireland may live on,
Polemics issue from a gun,
Vision lay booby traps, a bomb
Explode and to a child bring home
A dead man's dream of things to come.
Yes, granted, Yeats, in poems all
Our questions are rhetorical —
Until the pragmatists barge in,
Let loose destruction with a grin
Or cold intentness, the set jaws
Of jobs well done to serve the cause.
Terrible beauty? What prowls again
Is random murder, meaningless pain.

But, Yeats, you'd not have ridden out
The rough sectarian roundabout.
No, it's the cruelty of art
I blame for your ambiguous part,
A wilful, obstinate projection
Of art's prerogative, perfection,
To where it fills a bag of tricks,
The gadgetry of politics,
And rival demagogues will sell
Cheap tickets to the selfsame hell,
More cunningly will prophesy
What suits them, casting a cold eye
On life, on death, the poor fools pressed
Into ideal self-interest.
If contemplating minds succumb
To coldness, sensitive hearts grow numb,
It is from learning still anew
That there is nothing they can do
To break that circle, but withdraw
To purer air, a stricter law.
Our very vehicle is brittle.
Too much distraction or too little

Can cause a breakdown on the way;
And for arrival, too, we pay.

III

And so do I, dear friends and hosts
In Ireland, for my game with ghosts —
Ghosts you have lived with, and have laid —
By generality betrayed
And punished, even while I played.
Worse, after trotting round this course,
Mere tourist, on a borrowed horse,
I can't get off it now, until
It throws me, sensing, as it will,
The stiff imposture of a skill
Outgrown, discarded. Not for us
The harp, the lyre, a Pegasus
That won't touch down! But there's a chance
Some spark will leap from ignorance,
My meddling, partly tongue-in-cheek,
Yet serious, in a fierce mystique.
Enough, if like your corvine birds
They croak and caw and cry, these words;
Or chatter — since they cannot sing —
Unanswered and unanswering.

Recessional

How they pile up, your word gadgets,
Your sound-image-sense contraptions,
In containers, in stores, in dumps!
Each, for a day or two, advertised
As the most refined, indispensable,
Yet the cheapest, for all that, ever.
Then redundant, obsolete, stacked,
Just in case, when such is the pace of improvements
That lines out of date a decade ago
May come back as antiques.

Too much of anything, though,
Risks consumer rejection.
That's why our Music Programme,
The 'classical' one, I mean,
Between dollops of choral stew,
Tone poem fondue, symphonic suet pudding,
Treacly ballet suites with whipped cream
(So lavishly confected
By Late Romantic chefs)
Therapeutically interposes
Small dishes of verbal bran,
Dry as sawdust, but good for the gut.

Silence, I've heard it whispered
By subverters of our ethos
Of productivity, growth —
Which they call 'accumulation' —
Could be better still.
Well, the Shop of State, it's true,
Has many departments;
But you don't need a Prime Manager
To tell you what would happen
To the greatest of supermarkets
If it stocked a single shelf
With a commodity, silence,
Any housewife could make for herself,
Without effort, by switching off;
Without so much
As a do-it-yourself kit!
What's more, notoriously,
Silence becomes a hunger
For the one food we can't carry:
A food fed by silence.

If you think that's where you come in,
Think again, or ask your computer.
If you must peddle dope,
Blank sheets are your only hope:
Not to compete with the din
Could prove to be cuter.
Melopoeia? Goodbye.
Euphony? Greek to us.
Your novelties have grown old,
Like the horse-drawn omnibus.
As for your psychic tonics,
They're not even pie in the sky.
We have that — remotely controlled
By electronics.

Typewriter, cease to tap.
Press, do not spoil more paper.
Close down, give it up,
Joining what soon will be
The silent majority,
Unemployable, unemployed;
Even larger, more silent
When the ultimate detergent
Has washed us clean.
(Already it has been blessed
By the Church in convocation.
It's the dernier cri, you see,
In our salvation,
The nec plus ultra machine.)

To microchips and their feeders
Leave your primitive products
For them to process or scrap.
To nuclear technology
And its promoters entrust
Your residual property, dust
That would mingle anyway
With the silent majority
Once the missiles, undeterred,
Render Creation void.

One Noah and his police
In a bunker or outer space
Will fight on till there's peace,
Making sure that victory,
Briefly, is seen and heard
To be enjoyed.
In the end, too, there will be
The Word.

Conservatism Revisited

(with apologies to Peter Viereck, who had something quite different
in mind)

Is it a great house, opened up now for all
And sundry to gape at exquisite loot
Hoarded over the centuries, lovingly tended
By the skills of its servants, its devotees?
Well, in boardrooms this and that heir will sit
Lest the house perish.
                              But, no, it's a factory
Being emptied now of the men and women
No longer needed, when profit can accrue
Not from willing, unwilling hands but a closed circuit
Of instructions obeyed by automatons;
And money, grown parthenogenetic,
Can breed money from money for money's sake,
Fight money with money for money's sake.

What it conserves are its own machinations
Till, confounded by electronics too intricate
For atrophied brains and imaginations,
The controllers blow up the system. Its fall,
Demolishing houses, will level the great with the small.

VI

Needs and Pastimes

Poems for Adolescents 1973-1974

Talking to Plants

Isn't it soppy, talking to things
That don't answer back? Well, it can't
Do any harm. There are some who think
That a plant will respond, not in words
But by growing, with leaves and flowers.
Especially one in a pot, because
Like a pet or a pig in a sty
It relies on human care.
Who knows whether plants can hear us,
Can feel the waves of sound
Or affection? They respond to light,
They eat and they drink and they breathe.
And even if plants are deaf
It could do the talker good
Merely to talk; and listen, too, for the language
Of plants, though to him it may sound like silence.
Call it listening or looking —
When it comes to plants, they're one and the same.

The Garden Table

A dead thing, people call it. True enough,
It's fifteen years now since the living stuff
It used to be was sliced, hammered, hinged
Into the shape we see.
The more to disguise it or make it more weatherproof
We gave it a coat of red paint,
But took no care to cover or tilt it against the rain
That living it could have drunk.
It's brittle now. Through paint and into the grain
Water has crept, become its enemy.
Yet here it stands, on sturdy legs,
Even the top not useless. We eat off it,
Laugh when a sliver is left in our hands,

Could mend it easily still, with a plank or two.
For us it's as good as new.
At times we think there's much to be said
For such a durable way of being dead.

The Clock

I tick, I tick, and have no sense of time.
My hands go round. At intervals I chime
To count the hours and minutes that to me
Are meaningless numbers turning endlessly,
Because my world is one without a 'when',
Without a 'late' or 'early', 'now' or 'then',
With no events, with nothing to arrange
Or mark. Your time is movement, growth and change.
I do not change or grow, but for your sake
Inside me wheels revolve until I break.
It's you that move me. If you don't I stick.
You wind me up. I tick, I tick, I tick.

The Scarecrow

Stuck up? May-be. But not proud
Of the job I do for the Lords of Creation.
They stuck me up, dressed me up in their clothes
To police their field, their garden, their orchard;
Never asking me whether I have a quarrel
With crow, starling or bullfinch. Take away
These cast-off togs I wear, and you'll find
I'm a soft old stick underneath, with no power.
It isn't for me to weigh up
The rights and wrongs of my function.
They sowed the crops, planted the trees I guard.
And they too have stripped this earth
Of the seed, the berries that once were natural food
For wild creatures. I'm sure of one thing only:

I do what I have to do. Stand where I'm put,
In the cold, in the heat, in the rain, with a straight face.
If I could smile I'd smile when some wily bird
Perches right on my hat, before getting down
To a good meal. But that couldn't happen.
If they thought it could, you'd never see me again.

Weeding

1

Here I am again with my sickle, spade, hoe
To decide over life and death, presume to call
This plant a 'weed', that one a 'flower',
Adam's prerogative, hereditary power
I can't renounce. And yet I know, I know,
It is a single generator drives them all,
And drives my murderous, my ordering hand.

These foxgloves, these red poppies, I let them stand,
Though I did not sow them. Slash the fruit-bearing bramble,
Dig out ground elder, bindweed, stinging nettle,
Real rivals, invaders whose roots ramble,
Robbing or strangling those of more delicate plants.
Or perhaps it's their strength, putting me on my mettle
To fight them for space, resist their advance.

2

I stop. I drop the spade,
Mop my face, consider:
Who's overrun the earth
And almost outrun it?
Who'll make it run out?
Who bores and guts it,
Pollutes and mutates it,
Corrodes and explodes it?
Each leaf that I laid

On the soil will feed it,
Turning death into birth.
If the cycle is breaking
Who brought it about?

3

I shall go again to the overgrown plot
With my sickle, hoe, spade,
But use no weedkiller, however selective,
No chemicals, no machine.
Already the nettles, ground elder, bindweed
Spring up again.
It's a good fight, as long as neither wins,
There are fruit to pick, unpoisoned,
Weeds to look at. I call them 'wildflowers'.

Garden as Commonwealth

Excessive laissez-faire? Could be,
If dandelion, dock were free
To riot, rampage, rob, or smother
The delicate, exotic, other.
But are they? Well, this gardener finds
Great strength in cultivated kinds.
Peruvian lilies? Watch them thrive
In London, fight to keep alive
And, if you let them, soon take over
Like any willow-herb or clover.
Canadian blood-root, once at home,
Uncoaxed will flower, uncoddled roam;
And where the native flag has trouble
The Algerian iris roots — in rubble,
There, if you're lucky, to surprise
Your eye with winter butterflies.

Yes, gardeners govern; but not much,
And deftly, with the certain touch
That slowly comes to them from knowing
It is not they who do the growing.
Time makes them waiters, on and for
A chemistry at work before
Hybrid or graft had changed one stem:
What makes the motionless move moves them.

Names

"For thirty-five years you've been writing the stuff
You call poems, and you haven't as much as mentioned
A creature you've certainly met
In the street, if not in your own house,
Towards autumn; a creature remarkable,
Distinguished enough, not easily mistaken
For any other; the daddy-long-legs, I mean.
Dogs and cats, toads and frogs, even bats
Occur in your verse; flies and bees,
Lice and fleas, even woodlice, I seem to recall;
Slow-worms and glow-worms, and the common earthworm;
All sorts of creeping and squirming vermin.
That's odd enough in itself, but never mind.
Would you care to explain the omission
Of the daddy-long-legs? Was it an oversight?"

"Fiddlesticks. Does it make any difference,
What I name or don't name? Well, perhaps it does —
If verse does to those who write it or read it.
All right, then: daddy-long-legs, daddy-long-legs,
Daddy-long-legs. Have I made amends?
And for good measure I grant they are graceful,
The way they brush walls at night
With the faintest of rattling sounds, less obtrusive
Than the bumping of moths against light-bulbs.

But oversight? No. An impossibility.
Give any creature a funny name
And not the name but the creature becomes a joke.
Call the grey squirrel 'tree-rat', as I've heard it
Called by a gamekeeper, and there's the licence to shoot it
As 'vermin' with an easy conscience. Poor daddy-long-legs.
Even its Latin name, tipula, makes me think
Of tibia and fibula, bones of the lower leg —
Much as slow-worms made you think of glow-worms.
Through words we grasp things. To 'swallow a dictionary'
And digest it too, is to swallow a world.
Let's call it 'crane-fly', then, and begin again
With the insect that's carried its brittle legs,
Brittle filigreed wings across the millennia."

Escape

"Look, a white bird!"
She called out, at her street-side window,
But as it flew from the hawthorn tree
Saw the white merge
In pale yellow, the strangeness dwindle
To a common cagebird's escape.

Perched there, against red berries
And the yellowing leaves,
It had seemed white, an albino finch
Or some rare exotic visitor,
Yet in its right place, free;
Not mobbed by blackbirds or sparrows.

Identifying, she doomed it:
No bird hatched in captivity,
She'd learnt, can survive many days,
Let alone a winter, of freedom.
'A cage, and seed. Quick!'

But the bird had moved on,

Into who knows what harshness
Of hunger, predators, winds;
Out of our range too,
Safe from the lure of the half-life,
Ours, that we might have restored
For the sake of comfort, our own.

From a Diary

For G. and M.

Received the gift of a carton of logs
To burn when power and gas fail,
Coal and oil are scarce.
The fire will not last long; but the wood smoke,
More than the heat, will remind us
Of the senders and all that we owe
To the slow labour of sawing
Done where the slow trees grow.

In September

Rain and high winds. High winds and rain
After too little heat.
Pears prematurely fall, the flattened wheat
Will rot, the peaches will not ripen,
Though now through flurrying clouds brief sunbeams blink.
That's weather: useless to complain.
And much, much more is weather than we think.

233

An Easy Riddle

It rhymes with womb, with tomb, can be snug or cold,
Can oppress like doom if too gloomy, too small
Or merely not of one's choosing. (Some like it in halflight,
Some like it full of things, others of people,
Some now of things alone, now also of people,
Some like it bare and clean, some like it old
And don't mind dust in the cracks, reminding them
Of other times, other people, known or unknown.)
Some have many, many have only one,
But may like it the more for that. Some have to share
The one with people not of their choosing,
And all their dreams are of one of their own.
Many don't seem to care whether and how they like it,
Leave it much as they found it, feel no need
For changes, rearrangements. Others are always shifting
Themselves or the contents around: the discontent.
Some have none at all. Like wild animals, birds,
They make do, dependent on season and weather,
Sheltering where they can, alone or together.
A few don't want one even, have come to prefer
A life without it, breathing anyone's air.

Flying

1

Millennia ago it began
As envy of birds, of angels,
As a daydream of lightness,
The ambition to be
More spirit than flesh.
Long after Icarus
It was by wings attached
To the arms, an extension
Of bodily prowess,
A swimming in air;

But like Icarus all
Who tried it suffered a fall.
Boats held the answer:
Vessels were made, balloons,
And men became airborne, sailing;

2

And now can chase the sun,
Leave nightfall behind.
Can sit numb, dumb,
Reading, feeding,
Drowsing, drinking,
Examining memoranda
Or day-dreaming — of earth.
Can walk, talk
Within the limits of
A sort of hotel
That's nowhere, anywhere,
Of a sort of jail —
In transit between
Countries not even seen;

3

Or can look, weather permitting,
And see what millennia ago
No human being could see:
Himalayan peaks by the dozen,
A whole range of the Rocky Mountains,
The Grand Canyon entire,
Great lakes, large cities entire
And by night constellations reversed,
The twinkling lights of large cities
Neat as a map, made abstract by distance.

Oh, and the cloudscapes, arctic
Icefields of them, icebergs adrift
On a blue more translucent than water's,
And, in storms, canyons of cloud,
Cloud alps, cloud chasms.
Cloud columns, black cathedrals
More massive than any of stone, the sunbeams
Flashing amid them in shafts
Or breaking to brightest emerald, orange, crimson...

4

Were those the colours? They dazzled me.
Of a hundred flights and more
What is it I remember?
Not speed, not lightness, not freedom.
A falling, yes, in turbulence,
Like a heavy lift going down.
"Fasten your seatbelts, jailbirds.
Thank you for flying with us."
Contour maps of a thousand regions
Without the feel of one place, the touch, the smell.

In mid-Atlantic once
A housefly sat on my writing hand.
I did not brush it off.
I remember that common fly,
A stowaway, foreign there,
Winged, but caged in the 'plane;
Less lucky than I who, landed,
Could walk on good earth again
And, wingless, day-dream still
Of Icarus, angels, air.

Another Easy Riddle

It rhymes with honey and funny. Some hoard it
As bees do honey in hives for the winter,
But may find their store diminished or even replaced
By a lesser substance, the true worth of their labour
Consumed, and not by them. Such transsubstantiation,
They will be told, is normal where *it* is concerned.
For, seriously though we take it, have to take it,
When without it we cannot eat, in itself it is
A mere fiction, unreal; and the fuss made about it
The funniest joke in the world.

Those who know, or feel, how unreal it is
Prefer to spend; converting the unreal token
As fast as they can into things to be used,
Consumed or kept, enjoyed by them or by others.
Use is real. Consumption is real. Keeping
Is real as long as the thing kept gives pleasure,
The keeping is not for the keeping's sake.

And all keeping has limits. Time makes us givers
As well as takers; in time the hoarders too
Are themselves consumed and will have to spend
Whatever remains of their hoard, real things and it,
By passing them on; as often as not, to spenders
Who in turn are consumed.

In Europe once, in the 'twenties, the fiction exploded.
A loaf, a cabbage suddenly was worth more
Than a pile of the paper tokens that previously would have
      bought
Street after street of good houses. The loaf, the cabbage
Served the need for survival. The rents extracted
From street after street of houses devalued those houses
When the owners discovered the total was not enough
To pay for a single meal.

But the joke of it was lost on most of the hungry.
The fiction was patched up. Soon the hoarders were hoarding
As usual, the spenders spending, as though
A man could eat the numbers printed on paper.

The mere mention of it, and the fuss made about it,
One day will make people laugh; provided
There are loaves enough and cabbages and houses
And people inside the houses to do the laughing.

Politics

Much the silliest game that men play, it's the deadliest too,
Not only for the players. No crash barrier ever devised
Insures that spectators will not be participants
When the best of the best nation's drivers makes a mistake
Or is pushed, or skids, off the track. For the vehicle must be
Far too big for him, far too strong. It's a rule of the game.
But for that who would watch, mere cars going round
And round? Who would care, were it not for the danger
Shared by the public at large? It's the danger that makes
Those drivers more than themselves, makes them seem
        important.

Ah, but the deadly silliness! Some of those men
(Or women, lately) can hardly endure so much tedium.
They want more thrills, and only feel really important
If accidents can be willed. Where they have the power,
And in many places they do, their very first order is:
"Demolish the barriers! Smash them! Let everyone know:
If I crash they die. My car is the People.
If I swerve, look out! With my car called The People
I kill for thrills; and the killed will be people,
Mine or not mine." Then what happens? More often than not
Most of the crowd will applaud. Their driver becomes their
        hero,
His presumption their comfort — till their nearest is hit.

238

Round and round they go. Now with, now without
The protecting barriers. And never for long can enough
Of the healthy hear how the wounded groaned,
See how the maimed survive. An emptiness drives them
Back to the drivers, the track where one in the end
Persuades them that his race is theirs, since theirs is his
    danger.

Wimbledon on TV: the Ladies' Singles

The commentators clap their traps,
Then like a dripping tap it raps,
Heard from the next room. A brief pause.
More clapping, but of hands: applause.

For whom? For what? I make a guess,
Only to doubt myself, confess:
There's more to it than meets the ear.
Precise it may be, never clear,
Never predictable, this game.
Skill, practice, an athletic frame,
Responses quick, electric, but
Nerves that are steady, don't go phut
When calculation enters in
Because without it few can win,
Yet if they calculate too much
That breaks their rhythm, spoils their touch
So that they hesitate or snatch,
With would-be winners lose the match.
Spontaneous cunning, then? Yes, that:
The tactics of a prowling cat.
And luck. No tactics can forestall
The equivocating net-cord ball,
The little gust of wind that may
Put shots, and players, out of play.

And that's not all; nor tells us why
There's more to it than meets the eye.
Although they call them 'ladies' singles'
Two ladies meet; the meeting mingles
Two chemistries of hope and will
That interact, both mutable.

Add the spectators: mainly British,
Most back Miss W., but, skittish,
They disconcert her, laugh or groan
Just when she needs to feel alone —
The cameras being quite enough
To make the easiest round seem tough
To one who senses them. (She does,
And pays for it, begins to fuzz.)
Quixotic, too, they'll switch support
Whenever, poised, she rules the court,
As though appointed by the gods
To punish pride, redress the odds.

Guesswork's no good. I'll go and share
More closely in this weird affair
Which cynics, with a smirk, would bracket
With show-biz — as the tennis racket.
Of course, one wins, the other loses —
But how, is matter for the Muses.
To me, it's drama; tragic, too,
Tense drama, with V.W.
At once protagonist and gauge
Of energies that now will rage,
Now flag. The very way she moves
Transmits the fitful charge, disproves
Glib critics' talk of 'grit' and 'form'.
The needle jumps. She rides a storm,
A storm outside her and inside:
Fate and the Furies will decide
Whether her human gifts avail
Or, too severely surtaxed, fail.

Today they do fail — only just.
I can switch off. Indeed I must,
Thoroughly purged with pity, terror
By each successive unforced error.
Pen-pushing's easier, I think,
Than teetering on another's brink.
And, yes, to make my mood less dark
I'll play some tennis in the park.

On the Track

Leading or ten times lapped,
How slow we are, how slow.
How much of it is maintenance,
How much of it is patience
When, nearly spilling, round we roar,
Accelerate and thrill
Those who are standing still;
More motionless than they,
Seem to flash past, and grit
Our teeth against the urge
To break the circle, to let go, let go
And fly and die and kill.
What is it that says no —
What great inertia
Outside us — long before
We've traded in our skill?
Hands, feet and eyes transfixed,
Body and mind no more
Than functions of a car,
By that great circular
And overriding It
We're driven, and submit.

Later mere common greed
May keep us turning, clamped
To cogs that by our kicking
We work like circus fleas.
Yet once we moved; at first
Were moved to move, defy
The weight in us, the torpor,
Nettled, made keen by the need
Not to arrive, to speed,
By thirst — but for the thirst
No drink has ever slaked
Till tongue and gullet freeze;
And razor-sharp we scraped clean
Clogged parts that only wait for,
Fatten their own decay.

So, numbered, each lies down
In a tight, a whizzing coffin —
At best to rise again,
Relieved, from that routine,
Humanly crawl and see
The green leaves hang,
The brown leaves fall from a tree.

VII

Later Poems

Zombie's Notebook

I

September evening. Street after street the station of a long undoing. Whose house? Whose lighted room? And all those books? The thousands that 'I' read? Those pictures above the bookshelves: do 'I' know the painters' names? Those bits of furniture collected over the years, the mementoes, the relics, the ornaments — were they 'mine'? Will someone walk in now, smoking the pipe 'I' smoked? Or wearing the dress 'I' bought for her? Does my latchkey fit the doorlock?

'I' carry one book in 'my' head: the book of the dead. And see the hearse draw up, then the junk merchant's van. The life 'I' furnished is disposed of. Walk on, walk on, cry the voices, the known and the unknown, into other half-lit streets, past other houses. Your key fits no doorlock now. Chuck it into the gutter. — All right, then. But where do I sleep? They're such damnable perfectionists, the dead.

II

Must retain a minimal vocabulary, and mustn't forget to put on clothes, till it's time to take them off. When bodies couple, so do ambitions and self-conceits. The copulation of words. When woman compliments man on the performance, as women do these days, mustn't forget to reply: You also, madam, were classic meat. Minimal courtesy. And never: Madam, it's anyone's. A skill picked up in the street — oh, treasured, of course, scrubbed and polished, of course, of course. Refined by practice. But anyone's, madam, anyone's. Minimal vanity to be observed, hers and his, or the bones will break through and bruise them.

Remember history, too. Important to them, like the numbers of houses, like people's names. Never forget name, year of birth. Place of birth, residence, death. No, no, never death, unhistorical death. School, regiment, club. That's better. Remember membership. Profess profession. Assume assumptions. Put money in your purse: the small change of personality, however impersonal, interchangeable. Like the 'great' events of history that have made them what they think they are. Attend the latest play. Read the gossip columns. Or what will you have to say for 'yourself' when the silence falls at parties?

III

The silence. Takes me back to where I have been. But can hear the sap go down in the trees. Eavesdropping on nature. An indecent habit. Distracting too, when one's trying so hard to be human, trying so hard to be 'I'. Should be honest with them, perhaps, direct? Alas, I *am* different, madam. Lost, as you say. Slept in the wrong bed. Or is ditch the word. Naked under the hired outfit. Still cold from the morning dew. Not quite myself, as you put it. So romantic? Right, if you think so. If you think. If you...She's gone. So many words, for nothing! Unassimilable waste matter that would have smothered this planet long ago if 'our' words were made flesh, multiplying creation by more than a million times a million every minute of the day. Listen, I say to the man who's filling my glass, the more than a million times a million dead are jabbering too. A good thing they're supersonic.

Did he understand? Looks pale and lean, 'alienated'. Why didn't I think of that, a term at home in the gossip columns. Could it be, I go on, carried away by the urge to communicate, could it be that we've met before, in the other place? My mistake, sir, but you have the air. Death-of-the-heart, don't you know, and-all-that-sort-of-thing. Death-of-the-head, you suggest? Not mine, sir, not mine. Head's ticking over nicely, thank you, too well, too well. But the head has nothing to work on, nothing to propel. How about yours — the gearbox, I mean? You're in full career? Good for you. My mistake, I repeat. Pardon the verbal hold-up.

IV

Out again. Into the reliable halflight of the streets. A little operation, mnemochotomy, could still make a man of me. Dope and drink don't go deep enough, stop short on the lethal brink. And asleep I'm at their mercy, my familiars and loved ones, who are merciless, calling with voices like far-away fog-horns or telegraph wires in the wind. And there walks my gentle killer, asking me whether I'm well. Dispensing death in life, life in death. Never shall I leave you, she says, and vanishes.

A little operation, too much for the medical mechanics. One applied his stethoscope to my memory and received no message from the dead. Another's cardiograms and a third's encephalograms registered no abnormal vibrations. Simple enough — I antagonized Dr Needlesticker, the Nobel Prize winner world-famous for his experiments in neuro-fission ever since he made a tortoise split its shell trying to move to the right and left simultaneously — just step inside me, and you'll know what I need. Too simple, he replied. Grossly unscientific — and time-wasting. What do you take me for, a psycho-analyst? — Oh no, doctor, I tried those long ago, long before venturing to impose on your eminence. Forget it, professor. As I should forget it, if only you could see your way to that little operation. But who am I to doubt your diagnosis. Incurably healthy, then. Pertinaciously indivisible. Lost. No

247

matter. There's always the other place, with room for all, though its population grows prodigiously. — He was prodding the next man, a case of fingers inextricably interlocked, as if for perpetual prayer.

V

October now. Congenial time of the year. While there are leaves on the trees, the weather blows hot and cold, a poppy here and there catches a shamefaced sunbeam obliquely and burns, make for rural parts, going west. Away from the sham, to where all is posthumous, and mortal.

A pleasantry in the pheasantry: how human their condition. Hatched from expensive eggs, fostered by domestic hens that squat in cruel coops for their sake, pampered by expensive gamekeepers who nail the carcasses of badger, fox, squirrel, hedgehog, crow to branch or trunk as a warning to survivors that they too will be cheaply despatched, mature at last, in autumn, the colour of dying foliage but for the green that shines lasciviously against russet, feeding expensively, running, flying free, the brushwood, bracken, stubble full of their honking, scuttling, rustling, whirring — never to strut and rut in spring, to be pierced in mid-air from expensively hired guns of weekend sportsmen pampered by gamekeepers. No humbug there. Straight from the shoulder.

Into an honest night one stepped from the farmhouse. Capacious, cold, black. Shared with the heavy breathing of bullocks, shuffling of cows in the sheds, owl's hoot magnified by the sleep of diurnal birds. Brainless wind blew on leaf and stone, padded and bare bone. Trodden mud squelched. One step from light to dark, without so much as goodbye. From dark to light. Good night, night. See you soon.

Psychosis

Where are you, girl, under the whole hulk
Of smooth flesh unused, the figurehead eyes
Pale blue enamel staring, no laughter, no tears
To rise from within against lamplight, daylight
And refract them, playing?
Your lips are composed, for death.
When they part and the life in you finds a word
It is death, it is going down into sleep
And beyond, you're that far away, and there
You look for yourself.
      I look for you here,
Speak your name, beg you to stay, to wait,
For what, you ask, and I know
With electric currents they tore you
Out of your mad speed,
Joy of a kind, a fury, a pain,
And now with narcotics moor you
To where you are not.
      Why don't you die, is your answer,
As if there we could meet,
Or else to be rid of me
Trying to hold you, fighting
The undertow, tug of more than your weight
Together with it.
      But where are you,
Where can I reach you with words,
With tongue or finger touch you and make you feel
So that you move again, if only to drift
With the water and winds that are passing you by?

It's your self-love you have lost,
Unloving, and I cannot serve it unloved.
Yet listen for once, tell me
What the place is like where diminished
You long to be less. Let the telling
Cut you loose for your own way.

The Glade

1

All day in the glare, on the salt lake's beaches,
All night in a fever, shaking.
That's done with. My travels are over.
Somehow I'm here: glade in a dense wood.
Leafage makes lace. The shadows are of it, in it,
The season is everymonth.
White sorrel around me, and white anemone,
Foxglove purple, strawberry red.
Apple shapes, pear shapes have lasted all winter.
And the snow gleams above dry moss.

You don't see it, you cannot see it,
Travelling still to a town the guidebook foretells:
How it is to have gone and returned and gone
And returned and forgotten to go
And forgotten the route and the place
And be there again, and be everywhere.

Stay with me, love, till my fingers have traced the landscape
On your body and into your mind.

2

May we lie there, you ask; and how long.
By the hour, for ever, on a bed leased
From the turning trees and the conifers.
Leaving again and again,
Again and again left
To the dark and the whorled light.

Can you bear the silence between us?
You're of it, love, you are in it.
I fondle the silence between us
When I touch you and when I have lost you.

So late, nothing can part us:
We belong to the glade.

Mad Lover, Dead Lady

Oh, my Diotima.
Is it not my Diotima you are speaking of?
Thirteen sons she bore me, one of them is Pope,
Sultan the next, the third is the Czar of Russia.
And do you know how it went with her?
Crazy, that's what she went, crazy, crazy, crazy.

Thirteen funerals they gave me when I died.
But she was not there. Locked up in a tower.
That's how it goes: round the bend
Out of the garden where lovers meet,
Walking, talking together. Over the wall.
No one there. Till you visitors come:
Will the corpse write a poem today
About his mad lady?

But I'll tell you a secret: we meet.
Round the bend, on the other side of the wall
Our garden is always there,
Easy, with every season's flowers.
Each from a dark street we come
And the sun shines.
She laughs when I tell her
What it's like to be dead.
I laugh when she gives me
News of our crazy children
Who've made their way in the world.

No poem today, sir.
Go home. In a dream you'll see
How they remove themselves, your dead
Into madness. And seem to forget
Their loved ones, each in his own dark street.
How your mad loved ones
Seem to forget their dead.
That's how it goes. No one there.
Oh, my Diotima.
Waiting for me in the garden.

251

The Sewing

There was no saying it, you
Found and lost in the time it takes
To open and shut a door,
How every stitch stabbed;
No uttering, crying out
The now, now, now
Without before or after
But what the now could have made.
Had I died there, then,
That would have been true;
Not to mend, as words must,
The break with a thread.

There is no telling it now,
Or ever, to you, though I must
In words that will break again
Only because I live, driving or walking
Through the streets of a different town,
A carrier for coats that need buttons.
And the now is never, never,
The corner passed daily, twice,
With a buttoned coat, to be stabbed,
Far off, the thread loose.

Here's nothing, then: true words
Turned into lies by the lacked act.

Love

It ought to make mystics of us,
This concentration of all that we are and have
On nothing.
But I can't talk. Though my life flowed out to you
In words, while you lay
With another, at peace, happy,
What's ink compared to the juice
Which, more promptly undeceived, I might have spilt
For nothing.

If we must fall into it, for it,
No man was luckier than the near-mystic
Who at eighty-two years
Poured his love out in pints of blood
From the heart, lungs, mouth,
And died on his mistress, in bed,
Before she could leave him
With nothing.

You I write, even now, as though
Having words left, tenderness, folly unspent,
I owed them to you still
And hadn't given enough
To nothing
When happy, at peace in your presence I couldn't know
That had my blood splotched your body, soured the half-lies
     on your lips
Within hours you'd have washed it off, clean and new for
     another —
Another way of losing yourself
In nothing.

Consumed

The fault was impatience to live, burning,
The fault was joy that flashes and strikes, burning

And made this hollow where now the creature
Hibernates in my heart and guts.
Not that I let it in — I have never seen it.
If it was there from the start
It must have been free to slip out and return,
Feed and breed, run across turf, moss,
Leap or drop from one tree on to another.

Curled up now it sleeps; will twitch, as though dreaming
But not budge. Sustained by its own fat
Retches when I eat, turns every food against me.
What protrudes is my bones. No bulge betrays
How the creature thrives inside me.
Yet women, warned by a handshake, look,
Sense the redundant presence, and keep away.

When spring comes the creature will stir, leave me,
The hollow hurt again, ache to be filled.
Joy will strike again, burning,
And finish me off.

Dust

1

Living with it, till the flakes
Are thick enough to pick up
With my fingers and drop
Into wastepaper basket, bin
Or bowl, whichever is nearest,
Must I recant, take back
My 'hymns to dusters' (unwritten)
Now that she they were meant for dusts

Another man's rooms? A traitor,
In turn, not to her but all
Those heroic housewives, charwomen,
Worldwide relentless army
Fighting the stuff with equipment
So various, intricate, fussy,
It scares me, as dust does not?
Dropped out, for good, from that unending campaign,
Their daily advance by inches,
Their nightly retreat by as many
Or more; the chemical warfare,
The cleaning of cleaning utensils,
Maintenance of the means of maintaining
What never can be maintained.

No, I'll revoke nothing,
Not even revoked love,
Things that dust blurs or dust
Blown away uncovers,
Awed, as before, by the valour
Of grappling till death with death;
But, tainted, feel free to prefer
The smell of dust to the smell
Of disinfectants, polish,
Floorcloth and mop, breathing in
Matter's light breath, exhalation
That mingles pollen with down,
Germs with ashes, and falls
On my brooms, my vacuum cleaner,
On the whiteness of pillow, paper,
Unendingly falls, whirls,
Drifts or settles, fertile
And deadly, like being alive.

2

And yet in a dream I see them,
The dreamers of reason, the cleaners
Humanly march to the coast
Of every ocean on earth

To clear the beaches, reform
Those flotsam-retching waters,
Their seaweed-killer guns
Cocked in the cause of order.

The music I hear, dreaming,
Is canon, fugue, ricercare,
No slop, no loose ends.
If they sing there, under
A cloudless sky, while they let
Pure sand run through their fingers,
The waves hold back, it is:
Veni creator spiritus,
Antibiotic, make us
More than the dust that we are.
Lest we lie too long in bed,
Day-dreaming, of night,
Of nature's way with our flesh,
Come, spirit, and destroy
What merely lives and dies;
Give us the dream of reason.

I wake to the howling of winds.
To darkness. I breathe dust.

Gone

Thomas Good: born Beeston, Notts., 29 October 1901
missing from Richmond, Surrey, since 20 January 1970

1

"The presence of 200 guests,
Many of them only waiting
To die, depresses me.
I have not had the strength
To go to London. But
I hope to leave
After the 15th of January.

256

If I remember rightly,
February is like
A little springtime.
The other plans
I shall put off
Till April."
               My luggage
Has failed me here
Against a room worn
As my clothes, my books,
Manuscripts thumbed
By indifferent men
And returned. How long, how far
I have shifted them
Across the frontiers, decades,
Only to bring them here,
Home, Terminus Hall
Where no one dances
To penny whistle or gramophone,
A decorous quiet obtains
And the wallpaper, worn,
Repeats in weary tones
Its admonition:
               Rest.
Give up your journeys,
Give up your jumbled loves,
Lady of Pimlico,
Lady of Beirut
Who in Oxford and Aix and Verona and everywhere
Smiled from a bus,
Nodded high on a horse
As you fluttered on
With your phrases picked
From an earlier dawn's adoration,
Skipped with a joy
Your churchy youth forbade,
When the coin was valid.

Well, yes. I spent my life leaping
From memories to plans,
From loss to recollection.
This room clamps me
To the empty space between...

2

Once more he packed. With meticulous care
Though his mind was wandering out to the streets of wintry
        London,
Loitering on doorsteps of houses demolished by bombs,
Faltering over doorbells that no one he knew could answer,
North, by the Midlands, to Filey "surrounded by landscapes
That enchant me more and more", south again to Sussex,
And over Channel, rivers, mountains, Mediterranean sea,
While his hands disposed
Diary, wallet, passport, tobacco tin filled with coins,
Things he had done with. Paid his rent to the day,
Put on his raincoat and beret, walked out,
Leaving all he possessed, and one library book, overdue.

3

Feeling that void grow
Best filled with earth,
In old age or sickness a cat
From house to thicket will drag it,
Under a laurel hedge, close
To the roots will sit,
Nothing more in her gaze
Than a meek waiting,
Alone with it and the air's
Hummed continuum
Ever the same, from birth.

Could he, tunes in his head,
Busoni, music-hall,
Words in his head,
Heard and read,

Lie down or fall, hide
From eyes inside him
Of his living, his dead?
To what earth, what water, where
In a city not pitiless
Creep into animal time
Unowned, untenanted?

4

"There is hardly a climate in England
That suits me; and where to settle
I have not the least idea.
I am not allowed
To draw my pension abroad."
And yet, to keep moving,
Mind and body at one
Till mind stops, body drops
Is freedom of a kind.
I cannot help it, this joy
That gathers me up to defy
The better judgement of walls,
Gathers all I have been,
All I have loved, and drives me
I don't know where, to rest,
I don't know where, to die.

Thames

Good river, it carries
Food for men, for gulls.

Beautiful river
This winter evening
It melts into mauves and greys
Tower, chimney, wharf,
A mirror breathed upon
By haze and the lips of lovers.

This afternoon I saw
My friend's face, purple
After forty days of drifting
Between cold banks, in the brown water;

And drove home, along
The Embankment where he
Had breathed, loitered, loved
In a haze, mauves and greys
While the refuse of gulls, of men
Slapped the black bulk of barges.

White-faced, but with fuel enough,
With food enough to keep going
Today, tomorrow not far from the river,
Still able at times to be fooled,

Down through the rippled lamplight
I drive, into real mud.

Ode to Joy

You're somewhere, they tell me, hiding
Only from me. When I say you've gone, moved out
They show me benches, floors,
Doorsteps, the stone of back yards
You sleep on now. Hint that I may have seen you
And walked by, no eyelash left of your features
To blink recognition and, blinking, be recognized.
Brag that they meet you, know you, have made you
Their mescalin bride, for moments deep and delicate as you
    were
To me when one house could hold you,
One mirror suffice you, one garden was yours
Even in winter, the last of your heelmarks
Blindly divined under snow.

Hide? How can you, so near?
The less he courted you then
The more you amazed your long-faced lover
Come from his black pudding dinner, his raventail party
Down streets where the lamps had failed, by being there,
Waiting in candlelight, faithful to him.
Could leave for a sunny country, lock up,
Write him no postcard for weeks, for a month or longer
And return with a present, unchanged.
He, for the shareholders, meanwhile had itemized that year's
    trading losses,
Balanced their total against the depreciation of assets
And declared a minus dividend —
Coolly lugubrious. He could count on you.

All right. We're older. The dirtier air
Blocks or thickens the waves you transmitted.
Computers will plot a course
For the homing of homeless migrants,
The wildflowers you looked for will blossom on paper.
But call on me once, as different as you like,
As briefly, casually. Caring so little now
Where you are, with whom, you will hardly notice
What strangers we have become. We need not talk
If I hear you breathe in this room, this world,
Light finds a shape to outline,
A body to shine on, to shade.

Roses, Chrysanthemums

It's late in the day, in the year,
The frost holding off, just.
In the garden you pick dry stalks, hardly looking.
Time to come in,
Time to pick flowers, only now,
And carry them in, summer and autumn bunched,
Toward winter, even the full roses' petals
In no hurry to fall.

It is a slow music we hear
Behind the wind. And the chrysanthemums
Are a slow fire,
A red so dark it glimmers and would go out
But for the yellow that radiates from the core.
Ruffled flutterings here, a harsh odour
As of wood-smoke, and there
Flesh colour, silky, taut in its bland breathing,
Linger and mingle.

Now. Only now.

Babes in the Wood

In Memoriam Edwin and Willa Muir

No, they didn't get out,
Nor did they die, then.
They grew up, learning
To live on what they could find,
To build shelters, fend off
Wild boars that rooted around them,
Inquisitive bears.

They grew old, never knowing it,
Holding hands, lisping
Love's baby talk
Against buzzard and owl,
The half-light of day
And darker night —
Till the dawn when he lay dumb.

Come down, birdy, she said,
It's a cold hand I hold,
And hold it I must while he
Lies here for me to see.
I am weak, I am old,
The damp has warped my bones,
I cannot bury him.

It was ants that obliged.
But birdy said the woman
Who found her way out.

'Berkshire's Ancient Man'

For Richard

1

He can't be walking there now,
His head, bird-like, stuck out,
Ever so slightly tilted
Not for looking askance
At the new housing estate,
Not for looking at all
At the changes, mattresses dumped
In the ditches along the lane,
Nor stopping, except to roll
A fag or, for less than a minute,
Chat with us, chuckle
Over the rare good luck
Of having survived so long,

Outlived his wife, his acquaintance
And his very calling of coachman.
Cars didn't bother him.
No, horses it was
Had done for his father, his brother,
His father's father before them,
All coachmen or grooms in their time.

Suppose that his luck held,
The lane is a lane still,
No car knocked him down:
Near-centenarian then,
A decade ago and more,
He can't be walking there now.

2

At the southern end of the Appalachians,
Walking in autumn, in failing light
Up the narrow trail to the Horseshoe Falls
And meeting horses, climbing a bank
To let them pass, I remembered him
And the name you gave him, a child,
In a poem I lost or mixed up
With other papers that may or may not
Be somewhere in boxes no one is likely
To look at till both of us have forgotten
The old man of Berkshire. Already
The memory of that remembering fades out
In evening light, the shapes of leaves
On the trail, the waterfall high up
In the rocks, and the horses, passing.
Such distances lie between. We do not walk
Down the lane from village to village,
Suburbs by now, nor shall again.
So, for less than a minute, let
Him walk there still, your childhood poem
Be found, and even the half-lit trail

Three thousand miles away, never seen
By you, connect with the old man
Wickedly chuckling over the luck
Of having tricked them, those deadly horses.

Gardening

I

Most of the time it's enough
That a green tip shows,
Confirming you in the freedom to see
The flowering due next year.
Even the bare patch, undug,
Could be feeding
Slow lily bulbs
You gave up for dead.
If buds appear
Be alert, lest you're looking the other way
When anticipation, met or surpassed,
Becomes void for an hour, a day,
For a whole week.
Novelties are not new,
Unless it was bird, wind
That brought the seed;
And finally
You may cease to mind
Whether of currant, yew,
The neighbour's columbine
Or common weed —
As long as it grows.
Nothing's unique
But sunbeam's, light's play
On leafage foreknown.
That keeps you working, waiting —
That and the need

265

For what you think you are bored by:
For continuity,
A place of your own
Where bird, wind passes through.

II

Ripeness is all; but
The apples and pears that last
Take longest to ripen.
This early pear
Turns mushy or mealy one day
After it's ripe.
And the earliest fruit to ripen
Is the one with a maggot
Busy inside, at the core.

To be slow, to take time
And what the sun has to give,
Not to fall
In late summer, in autumn gale,
Ripening, is all.

North by Train, November

Less private now at our tables, and air-conditioned
We pass through the counties,
More smoothly, though, and faster than when the wheels
Lulled with a stuttering beat
Of syncopated dactyls, then jolted, screeched,
And we were somewhere, even if not in a station,
Held up. So that we stared
Or began to break ice by grumbling.

And now? As far as the Midlands
A hushed introversion reigns. Then the loud joky voices
Hail fellow travellers unabashed: neighbours, each one,
With a right to listen in
Or mind their own business, sour-faced, if that's how they are.

266

But outside the mist thickens.
Do I remember this ancient factory,
Sheds now disused, the half-familiar names?
Here and there a green still in leaves,
A white, startling, of swans, gulls
Or a window-frame in russety brick.
Greyness damps water even, the mallards' heads,
Cock pheasants running in stubble,
This man with his labrador at the edge of a ploughed field,
Till slag heap merges in copse
And the sheep look sooty.

Between Goole and Brough, through air its own colour,
A heron heavily flaps —
Remembered, identified, as we pass through
And leave the terrain of herons.

The light in the coach and the banter brighten.
Time to turn from the window, blot out
The hints, reminders gathered from haze
And prepare to be somewhere, a place half-familiar
Where strangers await me.

At Lumb Bank

For Ted Hughes

1

Through Manchester I had come, missing
All but the last of those black palazzi
Built to convert the muck of a whole world
Into England's brass; in dereliction become
Strict mourners, dignified, their faces blank;
And on through the eastern suburbs, out
Past money's gutted cathedrals, town
After town with bulky ruins looming
Gothic over the muck that remains
Of so much sacrifice and so much labour,

2

And found the place, remote,
Its hard indigenous stone
Streaked not with grime but weather,
Leaf-shade, a silence broken
Only by birds and the dull roar
Of rushing water, down
At the narrow valley's cleft.

Thunder. The low clouds burst.
I went out, to see; didn't feel
The rain, but between the claps,
Flashes over the ridge
Of the wilder opposite slope
Heard the silence again, deepened.
Here cows grazed. Descending,
All pasture I left behind,
All tilth, on a journey back
To a virgin forest of bracken,
Self-seeded sycamores,
Fine grass, in tufts. And there
The two great chimneys rose
From sheer earth, as though rooted
Like the trees they dwarf. Towers
Now, coeval with Babylon's,
Being useless. Not even
Rubble recalled the mill.

Those chimneys too will fall,
Their stone return to the torrent,
Be rounded, smoothed. No matter.
Already the place is beyond them,
Gone back, far back, beyond ruins,
Half-ruins where, huddling, we
Put off the end of our age.
A place for beginning again
With a river, with rock, with loam,
With a stillness; and thunder, and rain.

Real Estate

For Anne

1

Weary we came to it, weary
With advertisement's weary verbiage
And all those inglenooks, plastic antiquities,
The cocktail bar cottage,
The swimming-pool farmhouse,
The concreted paddocks, the pink mirrors lining
That bathroom suite in the Georgian mansion,
All the stuff that, bought at a steep price,
We could never afford to get rid of, by de-converting.

2

'For sale by auction: The Rectory,
Standing in well-timbered grounds
In this unspoilt village.
A fine period house requiring
Improvement and restoration.
A range of Outbuildings.' Yes.
'A Garage'. Noted.

3

We went. And there it stood,
Plain, white, right,
Austere, but with gables, bow front
('A later addition'), hint
Of indulgence in curves, dips.
Large, but not grand, compact.
Too sure of itself to be showy.
So real, it amazed, overwhelmed you.
So self-sufficient, you wanted it.

4

For sale by auction, at a low reserve,
After Easter, the powerful temptation
Of realness, every inch of the house honest —
With the rendering brutally stripped
Here and there, to reveal
Rot of beams, erosion, cracks
In brick, stone, the sliding,
Minute even now, and slow, slow,
Down into older dampness, of the foundations.

5

Settle there, could you, dare you,
On settlement? Settle ('subject to covenant'),
Bid for a place become
Pure idea of duration, dwelling
Among rook caws up in the black yews,
The taller pines, near graves,
Near enough to feel always
Held there, beyond dislodging —
If the floorboards, only a little aslant,
Hold, if the roof holds, if...

6

And the gardens, wilderness
Whose high walls keep intact
The pure idea, *hortus conclusus,*
Her who reigned with her lilies
Over wilderness trained, restrained —
Graveyard, no more, true
For bough, blossom, fruit
Gone down into older dampness,
To rise again, fleshed, if...

7

If not, the dead in their graves,
Near enough, will be heard laughing
At folk who need so much room,
Such an effort of warmed walls,
To make a home for themselves, a peace;
And on their treetops the rooks
Join in, with a raucous guffawing.

8

Let's go, let the place be:
Too real for us to meddle with, pure idea of dwelling.
Not for us will the rooks caw
Or the gardens bear again flowers and fruit;
Not at us will the rooks laugh.
But anywhere, miles from this burial-ground,
The wide-awake dead can tell us a thing or two
About making do with our real estate,
The for ever indifferently furnished, poorly maintained,
Defectively fenced or walled;
About how indifference grows on us, and the chores grow
      harder.

9

Let's go, and revisit those empty rooms,
Occupy them in dreams that restore without labour
Any house you have lost
Or lacked the means to acquire; improve it, too.
One look, and dream takes possession
Of all that the look took in; and will work wonders
With ruins, with rubble, with the bare site,
Instantly will rebuild, instantly raise the dead
For conversation with you, for communion;
And where no root is, no seed,
Break sunbeams for you with the blackness of full-grown
      pines.

Grape and Nut Letter

to Franklin and Helen

A little act — picking the last grapes
From your fallen vines:
Concord, with a tang still
Of a wilder state.
Thick-skinned, large-pipped like scuppernong
In the South. Their flesh tight,
Their sweetness tart.
Leaves beginning to crinkle. The dark-blue berries
Ready to drop from their tough stalks.
A few dried out: too leathery for decay
But hollow, the skin become a husk.
Well hidden by foliage even
Where stakes had withstood the gale.
Trailing, yours no longer,
Half-way to soil, or to insect, bird,
Rodent closer to soil
Than the makers of wine and supports.

A little act — of appropriation?
Not now. Of acquaintance rather
With the silent language of place.
To be gathered, too, from those wilder fruit —
Hickory, butternut — in shells so hard
That no teeth but a squirrel's can crack them;
Which, cracked between stones, yield
Only a hint of savour,
Of their pith packed in grooves, for a squirrel's tongue.

Cryptic I'll leave it, untranslated,
That local tang and lilt,
With all it tells of the weather's ways
And refuses to tell.
Only thank the grape-vines that, fallen,
Still forbear to put out thorns; and half-tamed,
Will unlock their part of wildness.
As I thank you, for the little act.

View from a Back Window

Bay State Road, Boston

A strip of street where nobody walks,
Cars, between dustbins, illegally park
('Police take notice'), fenced for safety
With concrete, wire, against the two-way flow
Of traffic on the throughway. Then,
Unfenced, the grassy bank, with trees, a path
Where nobody walks but joggers run.
Still closer to the wide dividing waters
That hardly seem to flow, their surface ripple
Flattened, slowed down by trucks, a bench more green
Than the short grass it stands on. There
A man — voyeur of beer cans, eavesdropper
On engine rumble, chassis rattle, screech
Of tires, gratuitous inhaler
Of gases not his property — could sit
And, willing, strong enough to raise his eyes
On the far bank observe the two-way flow
Of traffic on the throughway; then
The tall façades, bare tenement, turret of château,
Factory chimney, mosque rotunda, where
Behind the blocked view seeing could begin.

Looking Back: Iowa

A decent provision of hills, enough to feed
The eye's hunger for curves; of rivers, of rocky banks,
Of lakes and of woods, enough, just, to remind a farmer
That not all is edible, far as his eye can see,
Cattle and corn are not all, with rabbit, pheasant thrown in
As a bonus from what's beyond
His acres, his ken; but when a blizzard rips
Branches from sound oaks not his world alone
Is exposed: an opossum, uneaten, lies
Dead under snow. And above all, before and after

273

Blizzard, hard frost, that sky —
Larger, more generous even than land's extent
And luminous now, in November,
As I rise to it, leaving the ribbed fields.

In South Carolina

I

"Who's Charles?" she informs the young white couple to
    whom she's lent
The house her husband put up twenty years ago
Between two lakes on the newly bought seventy acres,
And they don't use now. "Why, he's the very best
Nigger anyone ever had." The next time she comes it's with
    Charles,
She in her car, he in his, to pick the scuppernong grapes
She wants for wine.
                        Charles has a farm of his own,
More of a farm than theirs, larger, worth more, come down to
    him
From his family's last legal owner. At seventy-five
He makes hay for them still, the hay he needs, they do not,
Digs the white sand, harvests the crops he has planted,
Cantaloupe, corn, ocra and bean and yam
For them to eat.
                    When he refused to sell his land
To the highway constructors, a son and a daughter of his —
Five he'd fathered but raised many more — had him put in a
    mental home.
They, with two daughters married to doctors, got him
    released
Before it broke him. He struck those children out of his will,
Repaid their concern with the gift of a charolais steer
Slaughtered for them.
                            To save him cost them three 'phone
                            calls.
Already they live in town, would plant and reap only paper

274

But for what he provides, their untouchable keeper, the best,
The wisest, the last of his kind. The sun that sweetened
Fruit on their land shrivels the stalks, is shrivelling
Him. When he goes, their farm and his farm will yield them
No touchable crop.

II

Such lushness, between the great rivers,
Marshy savannah, and ocean
That on the old city's pavements
Weeds push up through cellar gratings
And seem to take root in sheer stone,
Oleander, camellia rise
Against walls in narrowest alleys.

Yet the plantation lies waste,
Acre by acre reverted to woods,
Hickory, pine, where woods have been felled
And channels cut through the roots for rice.
The last of the slave cabins rots
Close to the mansion of English brick
That's restored and inhabited,
Not even dwarfed by the live oaks
Coeval with it, each tree of the avenue
So swollen with three hundred years,
The branches come down again to the ground.

By the shallow waterway that once ran
To the ricefields a black woman stands
Angling for mullet, bream,
A jungle of shrub around her. The lawns
Are mown still, a tiny formal garden,
Laid out as herb gardens were
In Cotswold villages, vainly asserts
An alien trimness, primness
Against wild growth, riot of cruder sap
That dares to encroach, and before long must win.

If history had the strength of nature this air would blend
An odour of gunpowder, iron, with honeysuckle,
Lay bare the bones, dug in deep, of tribesmen who hunted
    here,
Sweat that dripped on to leaves
And human flesh converted
To coin, under the whip's lash.
But the house is gracious, the air sweet
As they slide from their car seats to view the place,
Admire, take heart while they can, the inheritors
Whose deadliest weapon is chequebook or telephone,
Whose monument will be of plastic, who fear most
That between raw nature, raw junk, no space remains.

Lisbon Night

for M.C. de V.

At one-thirty a.m. my friend gets through to me on the 'phone
To explain how he missed me at the hotel, I missed him at his
    flat,
And we make an appointment at last. The cacophonous throb
Of competing juke boxes in the pinball saloons has ended,
The cabarets down in the square have closed their doors.
Only motor bicycles rev and clatter; and all over the city
Still the twenty-one revolutions and counter-revolutions take
    place
On the walls. I begin to extract a silence, a privacy from
The repeated yap and whine of a dog in a nearby yard,
When not later than two or two-thirty, long before dawn,
This false alarm clock, a denatured cock
Shrills, irresistibly shrills again and again,
Ripping me out of a quarter-sleep filled with the alleys,
The pine, eucalyptus, cedar and fish smells of Lisbon,
Glaze of tiled housefronts, the slippery marble of
    paving-stones,
Mountainside follies at Sintra that out-moored the Moors,
Conimbriga's Roman remains, the plastic and onion skins
That outshone sea-shells on the beaches at Foz-do-Douro —

Rich, inexhaustible cud for a drowsy mind.
Only dream could have done it, thoroughly pulping the stuff
For its own polymorphous needs, like taking me to a palace
To talk with Mozart in Portugal, then on, with him,
To a summer skiing resort in the Dutch Alps,
Where we're met by…But not now. There's nothing for it
But to live, as the poor do here, on credit, making the best
Of expecting the worst, and where other energy can't,
For the moment, be drawn upon, keep going on coffee.
Insomnia, television — they're much the same,
After all, apart from the missing knob.
So, resigned, I wait for the kinder blankness of morning.

At Staufen

for Peter Huchel

1

"Too tame, too pretty", you said,
Sitting in front of your borrowed villa
Overlooking vineyards, the wide plain
That far off, when the haze lifts,
Outlines the Vosges;
Or, if you turned your head,
Closer, the mountainous fringe
Of the forest they call black.

Not black enough, for you,
Driven out of your true home,
The menaced, the menacing East?
Tamed for timber, tended,
Its nature trails
Pedagogically furnished
With the names and provenance
Of representative trees;
And the foxes gone,
Gassed, for fear of rabies.

277

Not black enough, for you,
On their hill, the castle ruins
Pedagogically preserved
With a plaque for Faust?

2

Yet the homeless cats,
Untouchable, gone wild,
Came to you for food,
One of them dragging
A leg ripped by shot.
Above the swimming pools
Buzzards hung, cried.
High up, from a tree-top
An oriole slid
Through its small range of tones
And once, once only
Flashed in quick flight,
Making oak, ash, fir
Look blacker.

Nor would you let
Ladybirds, butterflies
Drown, or be gutted alive
By the black water beetle
That ruled the pool.

Too late I skimmed off
A golden gardener,
And returned to my book,
Old-fashioned Fabre's
'Social Life in the Insect World'.
To find that very species
Observed, recorded there:
Its mass killing
Of caterpillars,
The female's nuptial feast
On the male.

I closed the book,
And kept the corpse
For the green and gold of its wings.

3

Dark the gravestones were, too,
At Sulzburg, the Hebrew letters
Blacked out by centuries
Of moss on the oldest;
With no new ones to come,
With the last of a long line
Gassed, east of here, gone.

Well tended, fenced off
From the camping ground
And the forest's encroachment,
That site was black enough
Even where sunbeams lit
New leaves, white flowers.

You said nothing, looking:
Slabs of stone, lettered or blank,
Stuck into black loam.
The names that remained, German;
The later inscriptions, German;
No stone, no inscription
For the last of the line,
Who were carrion, Jewish.

4

Yes, much blacker they'll be,
Much bleaker, our landscapes, before
'Desert is our history,
Termites with their pincers
Write it
On sand.'

But with eyes that long have stared
Into the dark, seeing,
You can look still
At the vineyards, the forest's edge
Where even now
A pine-marten kills, as it must,
Wild or tame prey;

Still can feed
The homeless cats,
Can save, as you must,
From natural, from
Man-made death
Insects that, brilliant or drab,
Are skilled, fulfilled in killing
And willing, in turn, to be killed;

Can write, still, write
For the killers, the savers
While they survive.
For the termites, eaters
Of paper, while they survive.
Or the sand alone,
For the blank sand.

Mornings

String of beginnings, a lifetime long,
So thin, so strong, it's outlasted the bulk it bound,
Whenever light out of haze lifted
Scarred masonry, marred wood
As a mother her child from the cot,
To strip, to wash, to dress again,
And the cities even were innocent.
In winter too, if the sun glinted
On ice, on snow,
Early air was the more unbreathed
For being cold, the factory smoke
Straighter, compact, not lingering, mingling.

I look at the river. It shines, it shines
As though the banks were not littered
With bottles, cans, rags
Nor lapped by detergents, by sewage,
Only the light were true.
I look at light: but for them, mornings,
Every rising's not-yet,
Little remains now to wait for, wish for,
To praise, once the shapes have set;
And whatever the end of my days, to the last
It will hold, the string of beginnings,
Light that was, that will be, that is new.

Conversations with Charwomen

1

If I'd spent my life alone
Or had my way in such matters
They'd never have taken place.
Irreversibly bourgeois,
Heir to the title deeds
Of an abyss impalpable and luxurious
As a gold mine in Peru
Which no broker can sell,
Nonetheless I've always preferred
To do my own dirty work,
Loath to call upon
Charwoman, charlady, cleaning lady,
Domestic help, auxiliary household fairy,
Madonna of mops, demi-goddess of buckets.
To do? Not quite: more often to leave undone —
Preoccupied with 'higher things', as they once would have
    called
My inheritance, the abyss, and the lifelong bother
Of trying in vain to get rid of it.

2

Well, they took place,
Those distracting conversations
About cleaning materials more strange to me
Than my unspeakable property
Could have been to her who was widowed,
Her who brought a small daughter,
Her with arthritis, whom it hurt to see on her knees,
And over and over again
About tea, strong or weak, Indian or China,
About biscuits, buns, cake,
Where obtainable, being delicious,
About the weather I had been too busy
To taste for myself.

3

So distracted I grew, so distraught,
One morning I nearly cried out:
Woman, where's yours? I mean your abyss.
Where is it? And how can I learn
To mislay it, as you do, for hours at a stretch,
For days, for weeks, for months,
For the decade or two we have left?
And how, while our capital rots,
Learn to believe in pennies?

Frothy questions. Each one of those women
With her work and her words refuted them.
Besides, the abyss is private
And the last thing I can afford
Is to lose my self-possession.
So: That's right, Mrs Williams, I agreed yet again,
There's no doubting that tea contains tannin,
A stimulant, a drug, if you like, a poison.
But it does cheer us up, as you say.

Mr Littlejoy

I

Mr Littlejoy rises on a May morning
To feed his pondfish, then his treefrog. His?
Nothing is yours, the weather says. Amen.
The showery season makes them rise to eat.

Sunbeams today. A dry sun-worshipper
He blesses dry fish food, then earthworm, fly
For being up and going down. Amen.
Small food for the small creatures in his tending.

Wind. Broken cloud. What is, is all there is,
The weather says, and he believes the weather.
Now scales flash golden. Later, blur. Amen.
This frog's purveyor will be food for worms

Or smaller creatures, he hears the weather say;
And, good, has learnt to answer back. Amen.

II

Mid-day is past. Mid-week, mid-month, mid-year.
Three quarters gone the century. Past long ago
My life's mid-way. (Dark forest? No. Bright city,
Open, abuzz, her wound, her stumps on show.)
And the millennium slimes toward its end,

Mr Littlejoy laughs, and prompts himself: laugh now,
As long as lungs dilate and lips will part.
(Something adhesive — lava or miasma —
Prepares to break worn casing. Laugh while you can.
Breathe while you can. And while you breathe, complain.)

Still the dreams come. Still in the dog-day drought
This bush puts out true roses, one or two,
Though mildew films the leafage, ladybirds
Cluster a gashed and fallen pear, to drink.
New hope holds on — fungus to rotten wood!

Dreams of renewal, reconciliation:
The estranged friend back, with projects, fantasies
Unpacked, spread out for you, as though for sharing!
A child consults you. A child confides to you,
The dreamer of that child, dreams that were yours.

He dances, dances over the withered lawn.

III

The sea, the sea, oh, to make friends with the sea,
Longs Mr Littlejoy, walking the wide salt marshes
Towards winter, at low tide. The hungry gulls
Above him circle, shriek as he prods a cluster
Of prickly oysters, picks the largest, bags it,
Walks on with care yet crunches underfoot
Mussels marooned in grasses, winkles attached
To sandbank, rock, then plunges a cold arm
Into the slime of a pool's bed, groping for clams.
That underground is depleted. He tries again,
Pool after pool, in vain. Plods on. The near gulls cry.
Peculiar gases rise. He stops, plods on,
But to his ankles, to his knees, no, to his waist
Sinks into mud that gurgles at him, holds him,
So fondly sucks at him, he feels, he knows:
The sea accepts me. I've made friends with the sea.
And, stuck there, seems to hear a siren song,
The moan of whales, as caught, as taped by his kind
On their kind's way across depleted waters:
Cow's call to calf, cow's call to slaughtered bull.
Whole cities the soft mire of bog, he marvels,

Fenland supports that drags one lean man down.
The sea, the sea makes me a monument,
Memorial founded on the wide salt marshes
To the sea's friend, recorder of her whales.

Dostoievsky's Daughters

I *Sophia*

Let us now praise famous men; and the children
Whom they begot
By the way, in a frenzy snatched
From the less carnal conceiving
For which we remember them:
Fondly perhaps, not without forethought
At moments, between fits, in the sticky patches between
Turning out copy — bits of *The Idiot*, for instance —
Against time, against better judgement,
To catch up with debts generously assumed
In a dead brother's name;
To bloat for a while those insatiable leeches, provide
For dependants close or not close, the helpless or feckless.
Let us praise, too, the women
Who bore with those men, bore their children,
Bore the more carnal labour, rarely remembered.

Sophia they named their first-born
But could not, for weeks, have her christened
In uncongenial Geneva, her mother too ill
To go to the pawnshop as usual.
'The baby', he wrote in March
Of the daughter not one month old,
'Has my features, my expression
Down to the wrinkles on her brow.
She lies in her cot
As though composing a novel.'

Ah, yes, paternal. But how could he know
She was composing herself
For wisdom, for moving on?
'So strong, so beautiful,
So full of understanding,
And feeling', he wrote again of the daughter
Lost, not three months old;
And attributed her going
'To the fact that we could not fall in
With the foreign way
Of rearing and feeding babies.'

Praising her now, the forgotten daughter
Wise before she was christened, before she was weaned,
With her brother's wisdom, Myshkin's, and the famous man's
Who fathered them both,
Let us remember: somebody has to pay
For goodness — the scandal of it, the affront.
Let us praise, too, the woman.
Between fits, in the sticky patches
The famous man suffered, paid,
But his brainchild, *The Idiot*, lived —
Thanks to her, the carnal mother
Who paid for less carnal conceiving
And paid for the wisdom, the fame,
And paid for his paying.

II *Lyubov*

Mourning conceived her, a black soil
Nourished her growth
But when she opened her eyes it was
To a kinder light, to a warmer day.

Love they called her; and gave her the love too
That Wisdom, her sister, had left unused
When she died, in another country.

Did Love thrive on that? She lived longer —
Long enough to see
A baby brother convulsed, choking,
Her famous father parted
From those he loved;
And see him crucified, nailed
Into his coffin, straining — year after year —
For resurrection, so that the light
Might be kind again, a day warm.

No, she could not be Love, but remained
The loved one, Aimée, forsaken;
Before her own blood broke
Must break with her mother, her country
That could not sustain her, since he was gone.

And wrote, the famous man's daughter,
Of doom in the blood,
Of a black soil, mourning,
Of a love that could not redeem
But maimed her, Aimée.

Gonzalo: Afterthoughts

A happy ending? Well, we might have carried
Corpses away, as usual, clamped into doom's
Machinery. Back to its element, air,
The spirit was released, and easily,
The poor forked animal, this once, not punished
For being what it is. No wickedness punished,
As though, for once, air need not war against earth,
Nor will impose a truce. And all went home,
Some to begin a day, with a new marriage,
With a new government perhaps more honest,
A little, than the last. Others to sleep,
Where I go, rid for a while of the urge to prattle
Of the good commonwealth I envisaged there,
Before we all went home, even he so close

287

To founding it when he was lord of the book,
Lord of illusions, godlike as our maker —
An island's, a whole world's — who now will sleep,
Known by his works, the authorship in doubt.
But can we sleep? He, I, the dreamer who
Dreamed us awake, himself a dreamer's dream?
And never real, though true, can our play end?

The commonwealth that never was lives on
As Naples and Milan do, or the island
Caliban has usurped. Awake, asleep,
The wise old man, the silly chatterbox,
Half-brother to Polonius, will make you laugh
Now, even now, at his cloud-cuckoo-land:
"No kind of traffic...riches, poverty.
And use of service, none; contract, succession...
No sovereignty...treason, felony,
Sword, pike, knife, gun, or need of any engine..."
Enough. The gist's familiar: innocence,
Love that lets be, a mind at peace with nature —
Your nightmare, grabbers and manipulators.
I who have served and suffered your designs
Know how you dread the dream; but melt in it,
Vanish, go down. As I do, into sleep,
One with the dream that was before I waked
And will be though the fabric of this earth
Yields to your blasting. There can be no end.

Old Londoner
In Memoriam Thomas Williams of Walworth

I   1974

It's a bad year all right, it's a mad year.
The seasons lead us a dance. All summer
Cold air streams clashed with the warm,
Cloud clotted with cloud across
An unreliable sky.

Now the leaves are turning, poppies burst into flower
But rain closes, lashes them, ripping the petals.
Bees, chilled or drenched into drowsiness,
Can't rise to drink. For once my chrysanthemums
Let me down, can't fill out their buds. Today
It's winter. Tomorrow it may be autumn.

Government after government fell —
Into confusion. New ones took over, confused.
Ends won't meet, anywhere. No,
Ends disown their beginnings, effects their causes.
So suddenly changes come, they startle the changers.
Nothing increases but prices, and they with a vengeance.
Who makes paper, sugar, salt
Disappear from the shops — and re-appear?
It's no good heckling the politicians:
They've run out of promises, let alone explanations.
The world has shrunk to a tea-cup — with a storm inside it.

I'm one of the lucky ones. At seventy-five
I can go out to work: odd jobs,
To keep up the old style that was always
Beyond our means. With time for a bit of gossip,
With treats, a tot of rum at the Market —
As long as it's there — a gift to myself,
Gifts to my friends, even to strangers.
Those were our luxuries. And they are still,
With few of us left in the street, few streets left
As they were when most of us had our feet on the ground,
Small though it was, our patch of it in the terrace rows.

That's it, then: making do, while I can,
In a bad, in a mad year.

II   1975

What happened? Winter. Went out for a drink, late.
On the way home it hit me — from inside. I fell.
Lay there. How long? Two coppers arrived. Thought I was
    drunk.

289

Dragged me back to the flat. Dumped me. Lay on the floor.
How long? Couldn't get to the bed. Couldn't eat. Nobody
      called.
I was going down. Then came to again. It was day
Or night. I was cold. Somebody banged on the door. When?
Couldn't shout, couldn't move. The banging stopped.
Another night. Or day? All the time it was getting darker,
Inside me. And now they broke in. Ambulance men.
Took me to hospital. Dumped me again, to wait
For a doctor, a ward. Said I'd have to be moved
To another building. A stroke, they said, and pneumonia.
But their voices were fading. Knew I was for it, the dark.
Name, address of my next of kin. Didn't want her, my
      daughter
I hadn't seen in years. Let her come when I'm gone
And clear up. Get rid of the bits and pieces
She told me off for collecting — ornaments, books,
All that's left of my life. And grab the indifferent
Useful things. Only don't let her bother me now.
Stick in those tubes, if you like. They'll feed my going.
But no more questions. Enough of words now. Enough of me.

Second Palinode: A Poet's Progress

What's become of you, mentors, tormentors, my built-in
      fathers?
Do you think I am old enough now
To fend for myself in this waiting-room of a station
On a line closed down and sitting there, chilled but
      undaunted,
Accustom my ears to the silence you suffered before me
Yet at one time could fill with your whispered commands?

Well you know, whether we like it, see it, believe it or not,
Glory is all that we can be after,
The makers of things a handful of brokers and buyers
Pretends to care about, when the market is lively.
That was your business, glory. That was your one excuse

290

For the loves and the friendship botched, for the walks not
        taken,
The kindly word never spoken, the little act never done
Save in your heads, when the door had slammed.

No, I need you, my masters, need your preposterous
        prompting
More than ever, now that no nonsense prevails,
What's what has been thoroughly learnt,
Our dance explained as a freakish compulsion
To stamp, to cavort, to leap, without moving on.

Pool, did I perpetrate? Snooker? Those are competitive.
Sub-aquatic, my foot. They make television.
But our match — so brashly announced, so tactfully cancelled,
With even the posthumous fixture in doubt —
Our tricks are the reason, our dodges all aimed at losing.

Promote it, then, ghosts, the only game we are good for.
Don't give up on me now. Get on with your haunting.

Post Mortem

For Thomas Blackburn

1

Four nights without sleep in his mountain cottage,
Four nights of climbing
Clear of the humus where roots
Grapple and feed and rot.

Four nights of writing himself
Clean into death;
And deftly managing, timing
A last intensity
To leave no loathed loose ends.
Bare rock-face, sheer.

All went to plan.
He'd finished the final draft
Of his tricky last chapter,
Transmuting the bitterness, blame.
Now verse, for valediction,
Thanksgiving, blessing,
His 'Morituri':
Not in his chatty manner
But songlike once more, taut.
And finished that before
The drug blasted his brain,
He groaned and rose and lurched,
Reeled once, collapsed.

2

Hadn't he noticed? There was a line
Missing. Couldn't he find a rhyme,
Or only a half-rhyme, for 'suffer'?
Did his climb go wrong after all,
The rope snap as he fumbled
At the ledge he'd picked for his fall?

He never was neat, my old friend.
Too late, too late I could offer
Full rhymes, half-rhymes enough,
As decades ago I would
When he sent me his scrawls,
Who was gruffer, rougher by far
Than he could bear to be
And made himself, for the end.
That marred the symmetry,
That blocked the fulfilling echo:
How he willed his way of dying,
Forced and bent his verse
Into a gentleness, grimly,
Into a brightness, darkly.

In the flaw lies the rightness,
What he could not will, but was,
On the slopes, among scrub and scree.
And there I can see him, there.

Let 'suffer' hang in the air.

The Door

For Jorge Guillén

Wife, daughter, granddaughter,
How they tip-toed by
Lest the wall of words crack,
The daily stanza let in
Worrying love or the errands
It goes on, hurrying, daily.

All the more strongly you built
For the door you kept open always,
For those feet, brushing
Familiar boards, for the breath
Hardly heard, sensed,
Tatters of talk from downstairs.

In the room of words they mingled
With the winds from far-off Spain,
Fainter voices, footfalls,
Breath long ago spent;
And went, into other winds,
To places known or unknown

Out of each stanza, closed,
Through the same open door
On errands all quiet, all light.
There you are, in that room
And, near and far, remain —
The more for hushed love.

Foreign Fall

How did you spend them, all those months and weeks?

And days and hours and minutes? They spent me.
Now massed, now one by one, down the long avenues
Cars flowed, flowed in and out, or stopped, or parked.
Throughout September, above the roofs of cars
Butterflies, monarchs, flapped wings all art nouveau
To flee, still to migrate, by panic or suction changed
To hovercraft until, released, they flopped
On to a shrub, if any, on to tarmac, and died.

OK. OK. Inside the cars were men
Or women, doubtless, children perhaps, who went
Where human beings go, about their business. Right?
And so did you. So did the butterflies.

In other streets, anachronistically,
Were those who moved their legs, slowly or fast.
And there were those, the winos and the bums,
Who at the bus stop, in the shelter, waited
Not for the bus, for nothing to explode,
And they together with it, into meaning...

Ha ha, your fellow existentialists.

They sat, they lounged, they sprawled. They staggered, fell
And cracked their heads. They crumpled with mere waiting.

Ah. But the clouds were serious? And the sky
Glowed with true light, flashed back from highrise glass?
At times, in outer suburbs, a star was glimpsed?
And in museums glittered the detritus
Of unrepeatable seasons, fuller lives?
You did not go?

I went about my business,
A not-being-there. I looked and did not see.
I walked where I was not. Talked, and could hear
The words hit walls and ricochet, heard words
Sent out to meet them, miss, hang in mid-air.

And blamed the blankness in yourself, the block?
Loitered in graveyards? Resorted to holy books?

To broken beer bottles, rather, bags of garbage
Dumped on the sidewalks, under leaves that flapped
In various winds until by dropping they
Made known the month, October, then November.
In their own time they lay, dismissed from use,
The shards to sparkle, soft refuse to decay;
And that was freedom there, was luxury —

Before the obliterating mercy, snow...

Birthday

A shovel scrapes over stone or concrete.
Cars drone. A child's voice rises
Above the hubbub of nameless play.

An afternoon in August. I lie drowsing
On the garden bench. Fifty years melt
In the hot air that transmits
The sounds of happenings whose place and nature
Hang there, hover. That's how it was
For the baby laid down on a balcony
At siesta time in a distant city;
And is here, now. The known and the seen
Fall away. A space opens,
Fills with the hum, the thrumming of what
I am not; the screams, too, the screeching;
Becomes the sum of my life, a home
I cannot inhabit — with the sparrows even
Mute this month, all commotion human.

Elsewhere, my mother at eighty-eight
Lies on a deck chair, drowning
In that same space. Were my father alive
Today he'd be ninety, the tissue
Undone in him larger by thirty-five years;
But the sounds and the silence round him
The same; here, to receive him, the space.

A train rattles by. A drill, far off,
Throbs. A cup falls, shatters.

At Home

For my mother, at the age of 90

Early June. In a heatwave London is loosened.
Over fences, brick walls grown lighter
Wandering tendrils play.
Tourists are out, adrift, briefly to live by looking.

You're there; and your eyes can see:
Shapes you have handled, features the years have sharpened.
Your gaze cannot hold them for long. They will not stay,
Tugged away from you — into what?
A duration like music's you enter and leave, estranged.

You're there, but not in your garden.
Wisteria fragrance
Blows in through french windows half-open.
No need to rise from your bed or your chair:

Without looking you know how the weeds are taking over,
The last of your gardeners gone;
How convolvulus buds on the smothered gooseberry bushes
And soon will blatantly flower.

Still disorder hurts you. Your body, by hurting more,
Tells you each day to let go.
And the house, too, withdraws from your rule and possession.

296

Things have been shifted. If now you recall and wonder
Where it might be, your grandmother's tablecloth —
So devoutly embroidered and fringed
That all those decades devoutly you must preserve it —
For the giving away you summon the ghost of a care.

London, limbered or cold, has changed and receded:
In districts you cannot envisage your grandchildren lodge.
Yet they come to you; and you're there,
And can see them and listen — till their voices drop out of
    your time;

Into what? — A movement like music's
That reaching out to its limits arrives there only
To rest at the home of its range.

And that's where you are — your smile alone will concede it —
While, beyond you, your house dissolves.

A Silence

In Memoriam L.M.H., 1887-1980

I

The mellow light once more: late August.
Mat light on a fulness of leaves
About to die back, and a few slow flowers
She's finished with now but, newly widowed, saw
Four decades ago, in a different garden,
A street war had emptied;
And again and again before
She gave in at last, going
Between night and daybreak, between
Two anniversaries,
Of widowhood, wedding.

297

Little her care could maintain but the flowers' recurrence.
Nor that much, when last
She sat in her garden, looking
Past care at the flowerbeds, changed
In recurrent light, estranged;
And could not, would not see
Her fruit trees lopped down
To the bare trunks, all their branchwork heaped
In the farthest corner, for burning.
The light it was that remained, only the light.

II

"Take me home, let me go home",
She demanded, implored on her chair,
Her bed, in the same room
That was drifting now in a time-stream
Reversed, away, away.
Or set out in mind
For a party thrown for her by the past,
With Mama and Papa there
To save her at last from the hostess,
A psychiatrist who had picked on her,
Wouldn't let her leave,
Probed with impertinent questions.
"Naughty girl", said the nurse,
Removing her telephone
When she reached out to ring
The house that was truly hers,
The other house down the street
With the other bed, hers truly,
That waited there, never used
But made up, for rest.

Yet grief was falling away,
Anger could grip nothing,
So helpless she was, even love
Must turn back, to the root
And, far from the limbs, lie dormant.
What remained was laughter, driven through pain,
In a gasp she could prove herself:
Laughing at love that could do nothing,
That must give up at last, go.

III

Dial the number of her locked house
Where the brick holds,
Leaves breathe, roots drink;
And silences opened, the room rang hollow
Between reassurances then,
As by millimetres she slid
Off the thin wire on which alone
Bravely she'd poised a presence.

Dial the number and listen, listen:
To the hum or buzz, the high or low,
Broken, unbroken tone
Used, as words were,
Against silence, the gist, the gist.
Meet there again, where beginnings meet their ends,
Ends their beginnings, to diverge is to follow.
Listen, and never tell.

Migrants

Inside the house, betrayed by her heart and the bowels
That to her were indecent as death,
Lies the great-grandmother, brave and unwise till now
As robin, blackbird, bluetit alighting still
On her window-sill to be fed
With the biscuit crumbs that for once she can't rise to strew,
Chirpy always in poverty, widowhood
Until the tears all strange to her bird's eyes,
Human, welled up from a lifetime's forbidden darknesses.

Outside, we dare not report, on telephone wires
Martins and swallows have gathered,
Ready to leave, early this year.

Animula, spirit so little, so light
For so strenuous a flight to a place so far from the house.

Pavilion of the Brown Crane

(after T'sui Hao)

Long ago the wise man flew off, riding his brown crane.
Nothing remains but the empty memorial pavilion.
Once flown away, never the brown crane returns
Where for a thousand years the slow white clouds have drifted.

Now the sky is clear, clear the hang-yang tree's leafage,
Thick and green the grass on this island, Ying-wu.
As the sun goes down I wonder where home is.
Wavelets, haze on the river. No crane will return.

Willow

Hard wood or soft?
It is light, startlingly,
Not close-grained, to last
As oak does; but makes up
In obstinate wiry toughness for that
With all its fibres.
From the barkless bough
My axe rebounds;
My handsaw bends,
From the sham death
Willow, by shamming, defies.

Pick any twig, dormant
Or wrenched off in a gale,
Stick it in moist earth,
And it makes a tree.
Leave a trunk, fallen
Or felled, sprawling
Across a stream,
And it lives on,
Sprouts from the hollow
Half-rotten stump or
Takes root from a dropped limb.

Chop up the dry remains,
Burn them: they'll spit.

Beech

Starve, cramp the root,
Lop the trunk, closely set it in rows
And the trees will deny themselves,
Make a hedge for you, tamed,
Renouncing the girth and height
That, free, centenarian, in field
Or park they could swell to — their planters

Long left behind, outgrown. They will keep then
Their dry, brown leafage
All winter, until the crinkled
Ribbed silk of new leaves pushes
Away the deathly cover
No gale could remove;
Yet strain mightily,
Sideways and up, for growth,
Putting out limbs that shine
With a bronze lacquer too smooth
For bark; and, unless cut back,
Must kill or die, so straitened.

From the cuttings, though moist,
Live still, fire will draw
A joss-stick fragrance;
From thwarted, rotten tinder
Kingfisher flames, a flaring
Of brightest blue-greens
Before the white ashes
Let winds have their way.

Birch

Vestal she seems, ballerina
Of wildest, of waste places,
With an aspiration to whiteness
Fulfilled in America's North,
A papery peel so flawless,
It would shame the contagion of ink;
Yet rarely will attain
Her maturity's fulness,
Too often herself wasted,
Her bitter, her harsh timber
Stunted by what she favours,
Blizzards bending her limbs,
Long stillness under snow;
Will lie prone suddenly,

Crowded out, or as though felled
By a blow from her own boughs.
And proves brittle then, graceless:
Her wrapping of bark more lasting
Than the mouldered body within.

Yew

Too slowly for us it amasses
Its dense dark bulk.
Even without our blood
For food, where mature one stands
It's beyond us, putting on
Half-inches towards its millennium,
Reaching down farther
Than our memories, our machines.
Its fertile berries can kill.
Its dead wood even, still harsh,
In gate-post or bedstead
Outlasts many users
Of gates, of beds.
Woodworm, bedbug avoid it,
Those who used it said.

If one tree stands, black,
Where many trees were
And they whose counter-nature
For all things had a use
Till unburied their flesh littered
The used, the flayed earth,
A yew it will be, split,
Thrusting down slow roots,
Millennial, still to where
Soil remains whole.

Winter Jasmine

For a cold blossoming, less than cold praise:
Under veiled skies, in greyness
Eyes too are veiled,
And invisible almost against
A wall too much haze cast adrift
Nor weighty with fragrance as
Of its white kin
Or winter-white viburnum, honeysuckle,
To an absence of bees
It lavishly opens, displays
All those mock-suns, in vain;
Shines, but for senses dormant
Till aconite
With surprise caps its yellow
That fades now, dies.

Winter Aconite, Adonis

Not ostentatious either, long before
The trumpeted daffodils
Make spring official, but so small
That one must know the patch, clear it of sodden grass
To see the curled stalks bear
Furled yellow into still forbidding air
Of this last January day,
Opening only when the sun gets through
Or never, should the drizzle and the mist
Forbiddingly persist.
Furled or unfurled, foreknown or unforeknown,
By sheer anachronism more they will surprise
Than snowdrop white that's wintry to our eyes;
And before snowdrops may have come and gone —

Unlike adonis, built to last, defy
All sorts of weather, by holding back
The sturdier blossom on the sturdier stalk
For weeks, or months if need be, cunningly,
Leafage wrapped round it, and a tinge of green
Outside the yellow petals, for disguise,
Unfurling, furling, till true warmth sets in.
Then let the fanfares blare,
The pampered pomp of frilly daffodils blaze!
Its work is done, in frost's and wind's despite,
To put on death now, sweet
While all and sundry feast on the easier air.

Adamic

For David Gascoyne

1

Take your scythe to the flowering grasses
That winds bend, sunbeams wither,
And make a breathing-space for saplings,
For the fruit lately set on low boughs
Of cordon, bush the tall grass would smother,
Bindweed entwine and blight reach unseen.
The year's order it is, yours to uphold,
Salt of the earth, the choice is your own:
Relish the salt on your lip.

2

I go out and lay the good seedheads flat.
There's ease in the motion, both arms obey.
How else could I know the winds, feel the sun?
But more sure than scythe-blade the seasons rip
Through grass-blade and fruit and flesh of the grower.
Hardly he savours the crop he labours to eat,
Eats to labour again. Let up,
Law, for once, let one eye meet one flower
Long enough to see.

3

Now indoors, in halflight, a denser swathe
I cut, all time's growth goes down.
Soon sleep will begin to dig the garden inside me,
So deeply, no root remains but the tree's,
The first, last, all my work's undone.
Though seeing too well I awake, weary,
And rise aware of the bone-bare trunk,
Take your sickle to spurge, to thistle
The order will urge again.

Garden, Wilderness

Green fingers, green hand, by now green man
All through, with sap for blood,
Menial to it, gross nature,
And governor of a green tribe
No law can tame, no equity can bend
From the sole need of each, to feed and seed,
Unless, refined beyond resistance to a blight
More grasping than their greed,
Rare shoots evade the keeper's pampering.

He goes to referee
A clinch of lupin, bindweed, common cleavers
And stinging nettle — each with a right to be
Where if one thrives the other three must weaken;
And with his green hand, kin to tendril, root,
Tugs at the wrestlers, to save, to separate
Although his green heart knows:
While sun and rain connive,
Such will the game remain, such his and their estate.

More rain than sunshine: his green lungs inhale
Air thick with horsetail spore,
Grass pollen; his legs trail
Trains of torn herbage, dragging through swollen growth
Twined, tangled with decay.
For his green food he gropes,
To taste his share, bonus of fruit and berry,
Tribute for regency,
Sweet compensation for defeated hopes
Or dole despite the drudgery, the waste.

A garden of the mind,
Pure order, equipoise and paradigm
His lord, long far away and silent, had designed,
With bodies, never his, indifferent machines
To impose it and maintain
Against the clinging strand, the clogging slime;
And best invisible, as now that lord's become
Whose ghost the green man serves; that contemplated flower
Whose day of stillness filled all space, all time.

The Street, December
For Charles Causley

By inane innuendo he and she converse,
She and she, he and he, run into each other,
Exchanging as ever the message already familiar,
Safe in littleness, tucked away in discretions
And devious, devious, lest two raw wounds touch;
By local cryptograms of health, prices and weather
Conveying the constants, the universals of care.

May the Goodness that knows, the Lord that loves a duck
Keep it so, keep them so, never let them bumble
Into extinction, as bustard will, dodo did
In gun weather, knife weather, and worse to come
With prices too cruel for health.
May the drabbest, dumbest of birds and their words get
    through,
Zigzagging clear of on-target missiles.

Pré-Alpes

For André du Bouchet

1

Fore-alps I understood but meadow-alps we walked,
Lush with the many-shaped, the many-coloured clovers,
Vetches and marguerites, confusion of orchid kinds
And at the ryefield verges a foretime marriage
Of purest blue with scarlet, cornflower and poppy,
Though the wild sage could summon a still deeper blue,
Golden-eyed white was sweetest, gave out the heaviest
    fragrance
When wind or breeze ran loose among narcissus heads:
Persephone's meadows no farmer can quite possess.
His little herd or flock may crop the flora moist,
In winter munch the essences held in hay,
But mountainside, fallen rock, ravine where the spring waters
Creep through low leafage, gurgling, gather or cascade
Keep the man frugal, his narrow pastures rich,
Wildflowers outshone, outglittered by the wings of beetle,
Daymoth and butterfly, stone by the emerald lizard,
The copses loud with nightingales, roadside with cricket,
Sky with the buzzard's mew — in bird-murdering France —
Even the grass snake from the legend it will be,
If any legend can outlive the legend-bearers,

2

Last of these farmer-builders holding out
Against the silence of rooms too large
Under the vaulted or the timbered ceiling,
Too cool, too dark in summer
Under the triple pantiles of the roof
In homesteads long cast adrift
From villages that are names now,
Their workshops, stores, cafés
Closed down, the women gone;
And, hacking at sun-baked clay
For survival without succession —
No child's voice to be heard
From house or pasture or track —
On another hillside can see
A homestead's half-ruin
Abandoned by one who lies,
Unvisited even there,
In his walled family graveyard
Where, black, a great cypress
Lives on, not felled yet
By the land's new owners,
Indifferent city folk;
One who could not wait
Till old age imposed a truce
With nature, let him go down
In peace, because he must;
But cursing the grim love
That had kept him there, a loser,
The stubborn strength, his undoing,
With a shot broke the silence.

3

Stubborn too and alone you tend
Your plot of wild meadow, copse,
Making spaces for fruit-trees and old
Shrub roses; your plot of words
Older and newer, wilder and more far-fetched
Than those the market favours. A stranger
Here, but no holiday-maker, between
Persephone's presence and absence, between
The need that again and again wrests
From stony soil, from encroaching roots
Sustenance, celebration of harvest,
And the field all white with narcissus flowers,
Deathly whiteness, inhumanly centred
In the single unseeing eye. Your skill,
Then, at once to turn, to master
The matter, everyone's earth, and let
It be, give it back to itself;
Tend the plot, walk the hills
Less frequented now than the bird-crossed air
And in the forest, tracing what was a path,
Find behind scrub and one rosebush
What was a house, the strong rafters,
Firm roof pierced at last
By the trunk and crest of a tree:
A green halflight only through windows,
Columns of golden light from above.

VIII

Variations

Travelling I

1

Mountains, lakes. I have been here before
And on other mountains, wooded
Or rocky, smelling of thyme.
Lakes from whose beds they pulled
The giant catfish, for food,
Larger, deeper lakes that washed up
Dead carp and mussel shells, pearly or pink.
Forests where, after rain,
Salamanders lay, looped the dark moss with gold.
High up, in a glade,
Bells clanged, the cowherd boy
Was carving a pipe.

And I moved on, to learn
One of the million histories,
One weather, one dialect
Of herbs, one habitat
After migration, displacement,
With greedy lore to pounce
On a place and possess it,
With the mind's weapons, words,
While between land and water
Yellow vultures, mewing,
Looped empty air
Once filled with the hundred names
Of the nameless, or swooped
To the rocks, for carrion.

2

Enough now, of grabbing, holding,
The wars fought for peace,
Great loads of equipment lugged
To the borders of bogland, dumped,
So that empty-handed, empty-minded,
A few stragglers could stagger home.

And my baggage — those tags, the stickers
That brag of a Grand Hotel
Requisitioned for troops, then demolished,
Of a tropical island converted
Into a golf course;
The specimens, photographs, notes —
The heavier it grew, the less it was needed,
The longer it strayed, misdirected,
The less it was missed.

3

Mountains. A lake.
One of a famous number.
I see these birds, they dip over wavelets,
Looping, martins or swallows,
Their flight is enough.
The lake is enough,
To be here, forgetful,
In a boat, on water.
The famous dead have been here.
They saw and named what I see,
They went and forgot.

I climb a mountainside, soggy.
Then springy with heather.
The clouds are low,
The shaggy sheep have a name,
Old, less old than the breed
Less old than the rock
And I smell hot thyme
That grows in another country,
Through gaps in the Roman wall
A cold wind carries it here,

4

Through gaps in the mind,
Its fortifications, names:
Name that a Roman gave
To a camp on the moor
Where a sheep's jawbone lies
And buzzards, mewing, loop
Air between woods and water
Long empty of his gods;

Name of the yellow poppy
Drooping, after rain,
Or the flash, golden,
From wings in flight —
Greenfinch or yellowhammer —

Of this mountain, this lake. I move on.

315

II

1

A hybrid region. I walk half-seeing,
Half-hearing the mourning dove,
The mocking-bird's range of innate
And of mimed music, jumbled.
Here the dogwood grows wild, and here
It was planted, flowering pink
Above gaudy azaleas, in gardens
Carved out of hillside and forest.

Red clay. White sand. Meagre pines.
If no copperhead basked
On trails a Cherokee cut, no tortoise
Lurched over fallen branches
I might be back where I started.
Three thousand miles back. And colder.

2

Thirty years back. Three hundred.
It's the same earth,
With beer-can openers lying
Inches away from arrowheads,
Flint, and fossils barely covered.
The sameness confuses. If now
A rabbit screamed I'd be elsewhere,
By Thames or Windrush or Taw,
Moving as now I move
Through one death to the next.

On the one bank of the Bea,
Oak, beech, thickly bunched,
I half-see, on the other
Spruce, larch, for pit props,
Their thin trunks planted, with gaps
For a black light.
Over both buzzards loop.

3

By the Yare I called
On my father thirty years dead
In a city. From his bombed house
He'd retired, into a shack
With holes in the roof, gaps
In the board walls. Alone,
He was rapt, absorbed
In his new profession of nothingness,
And needed no calls, no concern;
Had forgotten so much,
I could not speak, looked on,
Looked around and left, quietly.

Still those words rot in my mouth
Which I did not speak, and others,
Unspoken, spoken, of caring,
For ever mocked as I stepped
Out of indifference fulfilled
Into a street, path, track
From which time peeled away
And yesterday's name had been swept
Together with yesterday's paper.

4

And yet I speak to you, love,
Write words for you. Can you read them?
Can you bear them, bear with me there
Or here, anywhere?
Can you keep them from falling, hold them
In a place become yours, real?

It's the same earth we walk,
Variously lost,
You from the dogwood, white-flowering,
I from the thin pines,
With many rivers between us,
Ocean between us, one.
To meet you I move on,
Sorting, throwing out words
Only so that the one
May prove sound, yours,

5

One place contains us, a whole year,
Our spring and fall, our growth and our dying
Be like your breath when you stand
Arrested, your eyes
Darkening, widening to reflect
And draw in, drown what's around them;

Wholly to see, hear again
And be here, there, wholly.
For that alone I walk
The named and nameless roads
Through tame and wild woods,
Along the banks of so many rivers
Too much the same till we meet.

III

1

No, it's over, our summer,
Part of a summer, you gone
Across the Channel with too much luggage,
Making your way back
To dogwood, red-berried now,
To nights warm still and loud
With whippoorwill, crickets,
And I about to go
Where maples begin to turn,
In half-sleep katiedid, katiedid
Grates out a brainless reminder
Of what and what, meet you, will not.

The sun has come out again
Here, in the same garden
That's turning too, never the same
One whole day, one whole hour.
Gales have snapped off
The last early pear
And, darkening, the goldenrod withers.
Over there it's budding, wild,
Like phlox, long withered here,

But without you where am I?
Neither here nor there, and the names
Dissolve, garden and meadow float
Out of my reach together,
Different, the same, both remote.

2

You move on, looking,
Finding something to feel
Here or there, anywhere,
Collect and lose, recollect
And like the more for the losing
That makes it more your own.
How you rush through Rome
In a morning, to see, to see,
To have seen, to have been
Where the names tell you you were,
Then, moving still, gather
What the names will not hold.

You got it home, your too heavy luggage,
Unpacked, and put away
Our summer, part of a summer,
Left again and for lodging chose
A trailer. You hinted:
An alias now was the name
That loving had learnt you by.

3

My travels, true, are unlearning,
An unloading of this piece and that,
Shedding of names, needs.
But the last have the pull of earth,
Of the earth we walk, our foothold.
Break them, and we fly or go under.

Almost the lightness came,
Almost the bareness in which
'The worst turns to laughter'.
I wait. The days drag,
Heavy, and long, long.
The laughter I hear is not mine,
My lightness no more than the weight
It was driven away from, a drifting
Between indifferent shores
Through this autumn now hot, now cold,
With the sky clouding over, clearing,
As if there could be no end,
Only the turning, clinging of leaves to stalk,
Of flesh to bone,

4

Though for hunger I needed your tongue,
For wanting to touch, your fingers,
For wanting, wanting you,
For looking, your hungry eyes,
For rest, their drowsing, their closing,
For bare words, your listening,
For destination, you,

Not here, not there, not anywhere
To be reached now,
So fast you rush on, away from
The place that, holding you still,
Could fill and affirm your name,

5

As I pack again, off at last,
For a while yet to travel,
Go and return, unlearning.

At their lightest the leaves fall,
At their lightest glide on the wind.

But enough now. More than enough
Of pressing into words
What sense, cluttered or stripped,
And mind leave behind them:
Mountains, lakes, rivers,
Too many, and you,
One, but moved on,
Nameless to me because named
You'd evade the name.

Here, in the same garden,
Branches are barer,
The late pears ripe.
No frost yet. Heavy
The grass droops, damp.
I wait, learning to stay.

322

IV

1

In winter light, walled
With glass too thin to hold
Any motion but memory's
That displaces no bulk, breaks
No surface, fills
No space, leaves no trace,
Litter or wake,

Travelling, stay
As Earth does, fixed,
And staying travel
As Earth does, revolving.

2

Earth. That must be the name
Still. Light. Air.
Walking the city I noted
That men live on light, air
Still, even here, unless
Filtering eyes or lungs
Fail, and waste clogs them,
Killing. The sun gets through
Still, the luckier poor can sit
On doorsteps, look up and see
A strip of sky they could almost
Feel to be common property.
A wind in those parts can cross
The river, cold, but bringing
Air nearly as good as new,

As nearly pure as the water
Rich people buy, canned.

3

Where am I? Bare trees
On a slope. Between the trunks,
Forked or single, islands of green,
Moss-green brighter than snow
Against leaf-brown, and evergreen,
Glossily dark, of laurel and
Rhododendron. Between shrieks,
A bluejay's, one call recurs,
High, low, low, low, the fall
Chromatic, moan of the
Mourning dove.

America,
East, with a little voice
Unfolding an emptiness, huge,
Though trucks roar through it, sirens,
Foghorns defy, define it.

4

And you? How near
In space, and more deaf
To me than my dead are.
So that now if I speak
It is of the emptiness, in a voice
Damped as the dove's in winter,
Of the emptiness only. But there,
If anywhere, you are listening,

Part of it, never more
Than half-born into place,
Time, from a region
Watery, leafy, dreamed
Before the cities were built.

Too late I take back
Those words and names
Of place, time, spoken
To bind you, to bend you
Awake. A mending, you said,
And left and hid from me. Where?
Awake? Or lost now,
The next quarter of birth
Too sudden, a wrenching, a rending
Away from the shapes of conch,
Pebble, tendril and frond
That moulded your mind?
Not to know, your need now,
To creep into what remains
Of sleep, not to be known?

Enough of grabbing, holding,
Of our fidgety greed,
Clutter that men dump
On to Earth, into Earth
Until no cure will work
But beyond herself
To unload, explode her.

6

Last of my needs, you
I'll unlearn, relinquish
If that was love. Too late,
Let you go, return, stay
And move on. Let you be,
Nameless.

Begin again, saying:
Mountain. Lake. Light.
Earth. Water. Air.
You. Nothing more. No one's.

V

1

Now or before, when the dogwood flowered
And you came walking out of no street or house
Known to me, with a gift
So much more than itself that the promise
Could not be kept. But the loan
Was mine, to consume like the air
Of that 'sweete and most healthfullest climate',
Yours while you walk there, changed,
Breathing its loan of air,
And the dogwood flowers
Where other trees grew,
'Great, tall, soft, light,
And yet tough enough I think to be fitte
Also for masts of shippes'
Of the kind sunk by sandbanks,
Battered by hurricanes there,
At the wild cape.

Gone, lost, the trees and the ships,
The possession and hope of possession;
Found, through the giving up,
Where I'm not, on the white sands,
A shell in her hand, she, 'for ever fair'.

2

I move on, closer now to the end
That is no end as long as
One mountain remains, one lake,
One river, one forest
Yet to be named, possessed,
Relinquished, forgotten, left
For Earth to renew. Move on
To no end but of 'I', 'you'
And the linking words, love's
Though love has no end,
Though words, when the link is broken,
Move on beyond 'I' and 'you',

As do his, who forsook the place,
His traffic island where love
Set up house and raised orphans,
Tenderly taught them to till
The hardest rock. Yet, after so much,
Gave in, to his blood's revolt
Against veins, against the heart
Pushing its dope, pumping
And pumping hope
Out into limbs that had learnt,
From things touched, to be still.
Could not eat now, the new bread
That tasted of flesh left unburied
Decades, frontiers ago,
Could not drink now, the new wine
That tasted of salt,
From a dry sea,
From a blinded eye,

And, slowly, began to go
Where he must, where
His poems had gone before him,
Into silence now, silence,
Water at last, water
Which, unclean, could wash
All it flows over, fills,
Even his mouth, of last words,
And move on.

4

Slowly, detained by love,
He went, but never
Slowly enough for Earth
In her long slow dream
That has not finished yet
With the gestation of man,
The breaker of her dream,
And has not finished
Digesting the teeth and bones
Of her dinosaurs.

Making and breaking words,
For slowness,
He opened gaps, for a pulse
Less awake, less impatient
Than his, who longed
To be dreamed again,
Out of pulverized rock,
Out of humus,
Bones, anthropoid, saurian,
And the plumage of orioles;
Cleared a space, for the poems
That Earth might compose

'On the other side
Of mankind'
And our quick ears
Could not hear.

5

Gone. Lost. Half-forgotten already
What quick eyes took in,
Quick hands felt the shape of, tongue
Touched with a name. Half-forgotten
The oriole's drab call
High up, on the crest of a flowering pear-tree,
A month or two back, not here,
Not in the city garden
Where from a drabber throat
A thrush luxuriantly warbles and foxgloves
Find a wood, though the woods were felled.

VI

1

Autumn again. Heavy and hot
Between rain. With a flowering still,
Belladonna, hibiscus, honeysuckle
While the leaves turn.
Around noon
From treeless pavements the sun
Hits back. All over them lie
Cicada, locust, moth
And butterfly, dying.

Neither frost nor gale
Hurt them. Their end
Was inside them, always.

But even on grey mornings now
It is birdsong I hear, and the dove's call,
Dark, not heard when I woke
To the slant of rays on to branches
Or brick. In all seasons,
All weathers, the first light,
Though less than the straight, lifts
A weight from foliage, from roofs,
From dew-wet grass, from
Those who slept.

2

There will be a second warbling
Before dusk, of thrush or mockingbird,
No matter now which, when the day's dregs,
Business half-done, half-botched
Beyond undoing, yes and no knotted,
Clutter ears as they settle,
To rise once more in dream,
Wildly churned, swirling,

Each particle a body, a face,
Now near, now receding, dissolved
Into flux and reconstituted
Only for more dissolution,
Mad dance within the mind
On a floor that spins, drops
And shoots up,
Till the hand held, become
The hand about to stab,

Plunging back too far, too fast,
Punctures the membrane wall.

3

Hardly one name was contained
In the dream fluid
Which, draining out, washes.
True, the awakening gives
Names to the shapes
Already gone,
In a silence nothing
Worse than owl's cry,
Train's rumble breaks.
Yet night belittles those dancers
'I', 'you', so that morning too
Is emptier, cleansed,

4

And at last it comes, the lightness,
Freedom to move or stay,
Be here and there, wholly,
Rid of the luggage left
In airports, railway stations
And locked up there, unclaimed,
With labels that peel, fade;
Forgetting to ask what woods are these,
What spider weaves the thread
Stretched from high branch to low
Across the path;
Felt on the skin, too fine to be fingered.

Knowing less and less, knowing
That to walk is enough
On the one, the various earth,
To see is enough,
The less lumbered with names,
The more filled with the sight,
With the light that's nobody's yet,
New, after all it has fallen on,
New, wherever it falls;

Needing less, knowing
That at last a rightness must come
Of so much unlearnt.

VII

1

So much forgotten. Care:
A furniture carefully kept,
Lovingly dusted, a houseful of it,
And passed on, in perfect condition,
For the heir to care about, care for
And leave to his heir undiminished.
A garden of it, endangered
By one week of neglect.

2

So much forgotten. As leaves fall
To make room for buds,

Food for the root that remembers
Leaf-shape, leaf-texture
When boughs are bare, sap lies
Low and rests.

Number, name alone
Are lost, reduced, fused
In humus. But seed
Remembers its kind.

3

Somewhere she walks, forgetting,
And the dogwood, scarlet here,
Where she walks is green.

4

No season now.
On the autumn, the spring bough
A mockingbird sings.
When rain comes down,
Wind rattles, wind soughs
It is winter. A dry stalk cracks.
And the bird rising
Flies into stillness.
If then a tree stirs
Wind has shifted, before
Snow blots it all.

Any season now.
When sun breaks through
It is summer.
There's a whirr, faint,
Intermittent, of grasshopper, cricket.
Sunbeams, through haze, draw
Copper, bronze, brass tints
From the wooded hills;
Green again, too. The air blends
Fragrance of sweet fern
With hemlock's, juniper's harshness.

5

I move on, I stop.
The chipmunk that shot for cover
Between rocks, creeps out
And sits, exposed.
We meet, eye to eye,
Where we can, in a stillness,
A suspense of ourselves in stillness,
Breathing, both of us, in a stillness taut
As breath held.

I break it, walk on
Or back, into rain, snow
That conceals and holds
Every colour, shape;
And without looking know
The buds on bare boughs.

6

Where am I? Here and there,
In a place my own
And no one's. The seasons whirl,
Halt. I question the air
And hear not one dove moan.

Let the rains wash
What they will; and snow fall
On all, over all.

Clouds bunch. A cold wind blows.
On the leafless tree
A mockingbird sings.

VIII

1

Or here, in the city garden,
Thinly, a wren,
Wintry piccolo minims,
Icicle tinkle, heard
From the house that was
Home. Or a robin
Twittering seasonless, thinly.

That much remains. While the walls crack,
Tiles come sliding down from the roof
And rot reduces doors
To a brittle screen, just holding.

2

Time to begin to think
Not of staying, there's none,
But of letting wheels roll,
Bow thrust, turbine suck in
Any air whatever, wherever.

With hope, fear? Not much.
Listening, looking still,
Not too shocked by the lurch
That fails to alarm, mocks:
To fall is one way of moving.

3

March. A swirl of snow
On to crocus, daffodil, primrose,
In earnest, it seems, for an hour,
As though come to stay, cover
Blossom proved rash and wrong,
To soak it, if not to freeze.
The sun breaks through; and flakes whirl
Single, slow, like petals
To which fumbling bees have clung.

That much remains:
Spring again, for an hour,
In the city that was
Home, but now forbids
A sense of return:
The remembered doorway
Different, the new
Indifferent. Both estranged.

4

Earth. Water. Air.
And fire, the sun's that sustains
Or fission's that sears, blasts
When other energy fails —
These remain, while Earth is stripped,
Ripped and chipped by steel,
Rain forests felled, even the sea's bed
Pierced, whole mountains levelled, lakes
Poisoned or drained.

5

Not for long will a bird circle
The place where the treetop was
And the nest. Once released
From the need, never again
May breed, but in his kind's unmaking
Only find rest —

Light now, light indeed
From such unlearning,
With earth to rot into,
Water to wash, dissolve,
Air to fall through
And fire, to burn in.

Estranged. By those global routes,
All curved now, all leading back
Not to the starting-point
But through it, beyond it, out again,
Back again, out. As the globe rotates
So does the traveller, giddy with turning, turning
And no return but for more departure,
No departure that's not a return.
To what? To a home beyond home,
Beyond difference, indifference, sameness;
Beyond himself, who is here and there,
Who is nowhere, everywhere, in a season endlessly turning.

IX

1

Together we've walked, and apart,
Over mountains, by lakes,
On sea shores, of sand, pebble, rock,
Moorland or marshland, on cliffs
Overgrown or sheer, through woods
Dark with leafage or dense
With bramble, scrub, bracken;
Down streets of how many cities,
On cobbles, on brick, on slabs
Always dabbed with old blood or new;
To look, to listen, to take in
And discard the dialects, histories,
To discover, uncover, a bareness
More lastingly ours; to return
And, dying a little, become
Less than we were, and more
By the loss, by the giving back;

If not moving, moved on,
Out of ourselves, beyond
'I', "you", and there
Brought to a meeting again
After difference, barer;
Hardly daring to speak
The other's name or the word
Of sameness in otherness, love;

2

To name a thing or a place,
Lest the name stick to a husk,
To a stump, to the gateway left
When a house was demolished.
                                                No,
Let the light record it, the seedling
That rises once more to the light
Where the parent's taproot was cut;
Or love's element only,
Fire, the last and first —
Let it blast, consume, reduce,
Propel, transmute; and create
Again, out of glowing rock-mash, an island,
Out of loose, mad atoms a planet.

3

For a while, though, yet
It's the wind, the sky's colour
That will bring us news. Today
Blackish clouds, blown, merge
And fray; their shadows race
Along pavement, lawn, chasing
Break-away sunbeams. A hint
Of hyacinth now; stronger,
The odour of soil roused
By showers, with last year's leaves
And wood-ash being rendered,
Washed down, mixed in, still,

4

Whether or not we see them, mountains, lakes,
The forgotten, the unknown, breathing
Heather or thyme, blossom of lemon or laurel,
Pine tang, salt tang or tar or dust;
Trusting the name, seek out
A roadside changed, grown strange,
Or await the turn and recurrence
Of mind's, of blood's weather,
Fragrances that a breeze
Blew where we walked, blew beyond us
And blows to someone, to no one;
Stop here, move on.

In Suffolk

I

So many moods of light, sky,
Such a flux of cloud shapes,
Cloud colours blending, blurring,
And the winds, to be learnt by heart:
So much movement to make a staying.

So much labour, with no time for looking,
Before trees wrenched free of ivy
Behind lowered eyelids began
To be ash or alder or willow.

So much delving down
With fork, spade, bare hands
To endangered roots before,
Weighed, breathed in, this earth
Made known its manyness
Of sand, humus, loam,
Of saturation, and so
Began to permit a tenure.

Landscape? Not yet. Even now,
Though more than a year of weathers
Has rushed, crept through the trees,
Leaved, stripped, torn off
Old boughs, snapped
Trunks of the newly planted.
In its burgeoning froze
This young medlar? Bending it,
Ripped the fine roots?
Other weathers will tell;

Let a dark red glow perhaps
Come again from the copper beech
Through translucent foliage, in May;
Deepen again the blackness
Of conifer woods, and pierce it.

Later perhaps, out of changing shapes,
A landscape will seem to grow,
Seem to cohere: a system
Of marsh and heath, of meadow
And forest, all veined
With waterways, roads. Not yet.

Winter. A night long
Gales tried the house. Rain
Found a way in. A gutter's
Jagged end hangs loose.
Iron sheets from a roof
Jam the holly hedge.
A telephone pole
Bars the lane to the village.

But bright the eastern sky
Breaks. Blue rivulets
Streak the grey north.
Mild or harsh, the day
Will be only itself.

Snow brings in snipe
To the sodden lawn
Pocked with molehills. Their bills
Jerk, prodding by inches
Down to the mud between clumps.
Now a tomcat prowls
The verge. They cower,
Motionless, merge in the cleared ruts.

Fieldfare alights, to fight
With blackbird, song thrush
Till a gull swoops down,
Then a jackdaw, to rob them and fight.
Only a lapwing keeps aloof,
Stalks at the far end.

Sunshine, a quick thaw.
And all are gone. A gust,
And even the sparrows, robins
Are not to be seen or heard;
But in the distance, wind-blurred,
Lapwing's, gull's cry.

II

Here weather is all, all's weather.
A spring has gone by, cold,
A calendar summer, cold,
An autumn drawn out, late,
With apples firm on the bough
In December, and brambles dropping
Berries as red, unripened,

Ungathered, too, by faltering senses,
A mind that waited, waited
For a season to be fulfilled
While the moments fell away,
The weathers turned, too fast,

And seeing once more was postponed
For a year, reserved for the formal recurrence
That, yearly, fails to occur,

When a long lifetime's years
Could prove not long enough
For seeing only, for learning to see
Mere bud, flower, fruit
In its own time, its weathers;
See it wilt, in its own time, droop,
See it ripped, wrenched, swallowed.

But now — snow. Intermission?
Nothing much happening? Eyes laid off,
Like hands, from hard ground
Under one cover, at rest?

Well, a gull or two veering inland,
White against white, the wingtips
Black as it dips to scavenge
And rises again, and dips.
A fluffed blackbird, hopping,
Stopping, tilting his head at the spot
Where no earthworm can stir.

And there's more to come, from a sky
White as the pasture where heifers,
Five of them, huddle, their flanks
And nostrils steaming. Aslant,
New flakes attack them, flurrying.

Intermission? A rest?
Time to look, to take in
Shapes the snow has reduced,
Suspended in sameness?

                    Already
Somewhere a gap has opened,
A farmhouse roof shines,
This blur reverts to pinetree,
Within minutes sky-blue has prevailed,
Torn clouds are swept on
Eastward,

                And light triumphs,
Glories in purged air,
The land's answering white,

That holds, yet begins to glitter
Crystalline with the greens and crimsons
Not of the earth it covers —
Of grass, dead foliage, rock —
But of light alone, silent
Emissions of fractured rays
Played off by the low sun
Over half a sky, against
Black cloud masses,
Changing still, at the end
Of a day, of a year.

                But before
Purple and gold go out
The new year's moon has appeared,
A thin sickle, faint.

III

In dull light it was,
In a thaw, after a lifetime of looking
At earth and water, that here,
By the culvert, a kingfisher flew,
Flashing a brightness that seemed
Not of the place, of the day,
Of the season, climate or region;
So briefly flashed, to behind
A willow trunk, that no gaze
Would have caught it but for the mind's
Long waiting: the colour, foreknown,
Was in it, kingfisher blue.
Iridescent, blue-green
And blue again, deeper.

Less foreknowable meanwhile the sea's
Weathers, moods, motions
Had encroached again, with more
Than the scuds — white mists
Drifting low across marshes,
Fields, and suddenly lifting,
Letting land be land,
As though created anew,
Cleansed and moist, glistening —

More, too, than the blizzards
Not even forests can soften,
Nor the too gentle hills;
Than the late summer hailstorm
That cracked and shattered glass —

But assaults on the sand cliffs,
Trees washed down, uprooted,
Cliffside steps demolished
And the remains of a clifftop house,

As a great city once,
Her docks and streets and abbeys
All swallowed by water;

And washed up, timber,
As the oak beams once,
From shipwrecks, that salvaged, carted
Far enough from the shore,
Made cottages, homesteads, barns
That withstand the weather still.

Washed up, amber
From the distant Baltic, bones,
Onions from somebody's garden,
Bottles from half the globe,
Bits of plastic contraptions
And oil, of course, oil
Stuck to seaweed, sea shells,
Drowned guillemot, cod
Cadaver: news of the world.

Less foreknowable? Only the sea's
Colours, shifting, mixed,
Its moods, motions. That freight
Curious perhaps in what it tells
A man about his kind —
Partly foreknown, after a lifetime's
Looking, moments of seeing,
Yet to be learnt again, always.

And what such jetsam tells
A man of the sea's kinds:
Whelk spawn cluster,
Cuttlebone, kelp,
Jellyfish of the sea's
Own and oldest making —

Made, unmade, still.

Not yet, though, or ever
One landscape, seascape, skyscape
But flux, only flux
To be learnt again and again,
Looked for, approved, accepted
Against the moment when seeing
Ends, because eyes have turned
Inward, fixed on a light
Less mutable, stiller, like that
In cornelian, agate, amber
Washed up on a shore, after winter tides,
And blindly the mind makes maps.

IV

March moon already, half-moon,
And the sky clear.
Wind from the west.
Melted, on banks, in ditches,
Last of the snow crusts.
By noon, after night frost,
Soil soaked with it, bloated.

Through last year's leafmould, a black
Sodden carpet, twist
Flowerheads on brittle stalks,
Sun-yellow aconite;
And through root clumps of grass
Thrust the snowdrops, moon-white.

Hints of a motion only, of a making:
How hard and soft, heavy and light,
Soil's dank, air's brightness,
Wind's bluster and water's weight
Conflict, interact, suggesting a season
That, veiled or averted, eyes will revoke
When sleet showers from the north impale
On their own blades the crocus petals,

And it's winter again, for all
The calendar's hopeful leaves
Or the willows palely greening
Where real daffodils droop
Unreal in the wrong air.

Two more moons, hidden moons of waiting,
Growth against odds, grim labour and preparation
With tokens, hints in plenty, day after day
That lengthens but brings no turning-point, no consummation.

Toads have coupled and spawned in the cold dyke,
Drenched, blown off course, a stork has circled the village.
Nettle, couch grass, ground elder as strong as ever,
A cuckoo has called, for minutes, and ceased to call,
Bumble bees, within minutes, have flown and retreated.

Birch followed willow, horse chestnut even put out
Crinkled shields round a clustered core,
Clenched nodules of blossom the chill arrests,
Pear and apple their buds that still cannot open.

May.

     And the dawns are silent.

          No swallow has come.

Ah, the airstream, at last, has veered:
Not relentlessly as before
Straight from the North Pole
It flows to demolish new shoots,
With gaps in the cloud, for doomed
Sallies of foliage, feather,
With intermissions of spring,
So that the collared doves bill
Without presuming to coo —
From the northwest this high wind
Spits rain, batters
All that frost has left whole.

If they could, the farmers and gardeners,
Now they'd give up. Go
To the shore: this way or that,
The sea has been in its element,
Changeable, yes, but seasonless
And immune. On the Dingle they'd hear
Curlew, sandpiper cry
As ever across the wide,
The treeless marshes, they'd see
The reeds, the sedge bend
As ever to any wind
Any weather can summon;

And they'd make their wishing slow
As the fishermen's almost whose lines
And nets from small boats
Bring in not all, nor much
At the best of tides, but enough,
After the work, the waiting.

V

And of course it comes cuckooing in,
Warbling, twittering, cooing
All the more for being late,
As though to make up in volume
For absent voices, the wrens',
Frozen, starved, despite
Their closest huddle in hedges;

Comes gushing into the boughs,
So that beech buds burst
Suddenly into silken leaves
That glitter or glow, ripple
In harmlessly wandering gusts;
And only with dew waters
So much outpour and uprush,

Which of course will not last as long as it takes
To turn from patient adagio to now or never,
All or nothing prestissimo, prompt greedy grasping,
Action, action before the frail tendrils break,
Small roots are overrun, small shoots are smothered,
The ash-tree's flower-tufts make way for more blatant green.

And again there's no respite, in human time, from the flux,
City time, with a view of one tree, walled in,
The season more sensed than seen, recalled or imagined,
Brought home by a summer frock. A room, in halflight,
Cool, for musing. On history, true, on deaths,
History's mark and measure, a street's meaning.

Here, weather is all:
To live, in the teeth of it,
As the birds do,
With a little always left over
For celebration. Or else
No longer to live, give back
One's cupful of selfhood to soil,
Sea water, fire, air —
Cause, once more, for a pause,
For celebration,

                    Until
A gale howls round the house,
Blizzards tear off the blossom
A year's care had pampered
Into its health, breezes
Had briefly flattered; and there
It is, fruition's doom,
A death, too, but one
The winds carry with them,
Utterly, to their nowhither, nowhere.

A holiday. End of May.
Swallows, a few, have returned
To sheds, furnace rooms, barns,
House martins to eaves.
High up, hating
To touch wall or roof,
Shrieking, the swifts mate
In wild loops, swoops,
Earthbound only for breeding.

Never this farmer raises
A face not worn but weathered
As the stone slab at the threshold,

His joys, his mourning grown
As hard and heavy, settled;
Attentive only to his cattle's,
His land's needs, his looking
An instant order to feed
Maintain, restrain, mend.

Yet more than he sees, hears
Is in his doing. He knows
The birds' ways, their flight
And rest; what's near enough
For naming, and what's beyond.
And when he rests, awake
In early or late light,
Feels the stone stir.

VI

Cool, a June turns
Into July. What earth could give,
Making up for adverse winds,
It has given: crab apples,
Reddening, hold. On the marshes
Meadowsweet, late, has pushed through
Furled umbrels above
Smothering horsetail, thistle.

Though in cool air,
Honeysuckle once more
Draws moths to its flowers.
The barn-owl's wide wings
Gleam white as they beat, glide
Over pastures in lingering halflight.

One who lovingly, long,
Laboriously had prepared his death
At broom-time achieved it.
He looked, and the petals dropped.
Now seed-pods hang there.

Another as long has hidden,
While in her body, not old,
The right and the wrong cells
Inch by inch fought.

Her summer, too, hides
Elsewhere: a haze dims
Landmarks the brightest noon
Asserts, or dawn proposes.
Rejected, they leave her empty,
Go to a gaze they can fill.

Nor this night does she join the fête that, for once, levels
Almost as death will, those divided by day,
Where the white-haired lady has clasped a child's hand,
A nonagenarian watches; but from the village green
To her cottage the music drifts: accordion, drum,
For the round, the morris dances, a wild fiddler's jig
And, for the young, a recorded, amplified blare
That reaches her as a throb only, a thrum
No more human now than the wavebeat heard in a forest.

A yellow half-moon, blurred,
Casts doubt on day-time limits,
Day-time labours. A scud
Curls over hedges, treetops,
Dense in the jaundiced glimmer.
Out of a cloud comes
Cattle's lowing, a sheep's
Bleat. What creeps in
Is the same sea, quiet,
That, wild, demolished a city,
Still erodes the shore.

Shortest nights. Too long by far
For her who lies between sleep and waking,
Racked, pulled this way and that
Not by pain alone and the drugs' half-promise
But the motions of sun and moon, tugging
At her this way and that, at war;
So that the first light, too, hurts
With a comfort at once revoked when she hears
The cock shrill, millennial, his call
To another day she will spend dying,

And, for sun's or moon's or for her own sake,
For land's or sea's, must let go, disown,
Yet be at one still with the dance
She is absent from, and the small hours
Break up, all the dancers leaving,
When for none and all the cock shrills.

VII

High summer. A weariness,
Whatever the weather, of leaf,
Of bird throat, of limb.

Late flowerheads, of meadowsweet,
Willow herb, half strangled
By convolvulus twine, dot
Marshland in disarray.

Early crop, second brood,
Second planting, patchwork
Of little chores relieve
A wavering equipoise
Between upsurge and fall.

If a storm blows now
Perversely it hurls to the ground
Live branches, unripe fruit,
With a bonus of turmoil, the sea's,
Gratuitous food for the hunger
Only of headlines and dogfish.

If the sky clears, a warmth
Hangs in the air, it is wasps
That feast on sweetening apples,
Hollow them out and drop,
Helplessly drunk, from the husks.

Consummation? If so,
A good season for dying;
For going away. On vacation?
Yes, into vacancy, out
Of natural time's repetitions,
Need, its remission, need
And the seeing to it, the remission
Again and again and again;

Into a city, built
To kill that time, to impose
Mind's mastery, freedom?
Walk there, on pavements
Half vacated now, half filled
With killers of empty time,
Come a long way to look
At the sights, memorial, museum,
Mausoleum — of what?
Of time once more, become
Money-time, dying,

Ever since in the squares
Heirlooms lost their innocence,
Experts pronounced the sentences
That put a price on ancestral heads,
To kill time once more, buy
A reprieve that is money-time, dying;
While in tower-block cubicle, in bed-sitter
Harder than murderous weather each walled day presses.

Sycamore: London tree, long ago wrenched
From a site bulldozers razed, for gain,
And concrete buried,
Measure once of the slower rotation
Cities deny; guardian
Whose green, grey and red alike made
A refuge home, though they darkened
The basement room that before demolition
Was reinforced against bombs;
And darkened it still
When year after year the house
Gaped from black window-holes into wilderness.

Sycamore: old in that place
As the stuccoed brick;
But rising from winged seed
In crack and rubble all over the city,
Even from poisoned earth, in the back yard
A factory overshadowed,
Oozing chromium waste
Under and into foundations.
From a thin stem, aslant
With turning in vain to the blocked-out sun
In thin light, shaftlight,
No blossom it could accomplish,
Yet leaves true to kind where grass had withered.

No, not now or in any season
The necropolitan tour
Through mind-mastered city time,
Along railside ruins and rubbish tips,
Through dockside ruins, for history;
Past the offices, shops, flats
Which, refurbished or cleared, expose
Discontinuities, relics of time
Running out, of money-time, dying;
For what the future holds,
Computers, the prophets of profits,
Calculators of doles
And apportioners of disasters.

Sycamore: here and there still
In its own time, straight,
With wide branches, it rises
And the shed leaves feed
Rich or poor soil, unpoisoned;

Close to brick, stone, steel,
Close to concrete, fills
A space its own but shared
With those gone and to come
Whose growth, too, is a reaching up
From the root's need into light;

Whose way is to fight time —
Time that the tree shares, time of their making —
For the mind's freedom, renewal
Neither spring nor autumn grants,
And accept it, time's tenants.

Harvest's begun. Already
Fires have swept fields,
Leaving black stubble.
Others are bare, turned.

Swallows in wet wires
Forgather their young, to rehearse departure,
Teach them to climb winds
And lie on winds, resting.

Cumbrous farm machines
Hold up the traffic back
To the cities, to work that will tick
And drag, repetitive, or will pulse
Humanly, in a broken rhythm.

VIII

Brooding light. The days muted,
Muffled, as though no noise
From fighter 'plane, truck,
No voice from village or pasture
Could pierce it, this wad of silence
The land's put on; no wind,
Ruffling leafage still thick,
Green or yellowing (silvery
White, upturned, on the poplars)
Could prod a tree to hurry
Over the business of fall.

Though as ever the air flows,
Freely grass and weeds
Grow, from new seed
Recently scattered, a circle,
Somewhere, is full, as the barns are,
The next not yet begun.

Michaelmas. Season
Of seasonless blossoming,
Ghostly; termination
Of tenure; removal; repair.

Silent through mat silken skies,
High up, the last martins glided,
Swallows and swifts gone.
From reedbeds and shores now
Slower wings flap,
Black arrowhead, to the south.

Dubiously day breaks.
A glimmer creeps into low haze
With the moon bright above it,
One star bright and the hinted flicker
Of other stars, too faint,
Too far for the eye's habit.

No thrush responds to such dawning.
Far off, a cock's crow, faint,
Merges in cattle's lowing
And is drowned in a bellow, a wail
That seems to slide up from the doom
Of their patient, their used kind,
Though a call merely, for milking.
Yet the stillness holds, stronger.

Towards mid-morning, a second dawn
As the sun breaks through, warm
Between black cloud-drifts;
But an introversion of earth
Leaves the day suspended.
Late flowers, late fruit obey
No urge but their own to linger,
Dismissed by the year's waning,
Fill a time all their own,
All aftermath, hushed;

And are most themselves in the half-hour
When even the damped shine
Begins to fade, their colours
Owe least to light's collusion,
Their glowing a cold fire
Kindled, fed from within.

The eye it is, wearying
After pale pinks and mauves,
Ghostly, of colchicum,
Michaelmas daisy, that bleeds
Last poppies of their scarlet.

The mind it is that withdraws
Into a winter, impatient
Not only for rest but the buds
On boughs not yet leafless;
Bent on its own rebirth,
Finds this dying too slow,
Leaps from fruition, store
To its greater need, hope,

To digging once more, in grey drizzle,
To sowing once more the turned earth,
While still the ungathered apples are gathering sunrays
On the tops of tall trees, and quinces deepening
Their lime to downed lemon, their lemon to gold.

IX

Winter solstice. Air
Takes over from earth at rest.
A hawk braves the gale,
Hangs over stalks that snap
Or fold at the base, mouldy.

Sky takes over, from land,
At sunrise, sundown bursts
Into a cold fluorescence,
As though all the brightness lost
To beech leaves that, withered,
Russet, remain unfallen,
To ilex, holly, fir,
And a year's whole range of blossom
Had gathered up there, to shine.

Here, only water
Responds to such light;
And fire holds its own.
If a kingfisher now
Flashed, cock pheasant
Nodded by, near,
At noon, yet they would fade
And eyes be referred higher.

Only in windless nights,
Damp, without frost,
By starlight a haze dims,
Still earth emits
Hints of growth in decay,
Cattle smell, care
And hope, smell of straw,
Hay, of wood smoke,

Rising too, drifting
Away, exhaled by fire
Into air, leaving
White ashes only
To be mixed back into earth
By water, and feed roots.

When heavy wings beat
In slow time, silent,
Trace the river-banks,
Measure a heavier stillness
And close, merged in mist,
A thin line, vanishing,
It is a heron between
Earth and water and air,

Effigy now of a bird,
Or signpost, fixed, that points
Out of its world and ours
Into blankness, extinction:
Blasting of all the ways,
All the kinds and weathers
By deadly fire, fission.

And in dim light on the village green
Round the tall spruce hung
With electric bulbs, in a broken circle
Faltering singers fumbled
For words that seemed half-forgotten,
Unable to rise against
Darkness not dark enough,
Silence not silent enough,

Since a loudspeaker purveyed
The finished product, sweetened
With a cinema organ's falsetto,
A confection of tinkling bells,
And prompted nothing, but shamed back
Into half-silence their voices,
Into half-darkness their hope,

Till the ceremony had ceased,
Till the words were not summoned,
Till out of the circle of light
Each walked back lonelier
Under the same star
To a house less owned.

For the moment, breathing clean air
That tastes new, renewed like the year,
The decade soon to begin, they look up
To the same star, can hear the words
Left unsaid, unsung, a music more quiet
Yet harsher, remember the hope put away,
The remedy kept in reserve and passed on
Heart to heart, with a whispered warning:
For external use only. Danger.
Can be fatal if taken internally,
Applied in excess or in the wrong place;

And, recurrent too, a dread
That the promise could be fufilled,
The time near when truth
Is exacted whole, stark:
No spring after winter,
No growth from any sowing,
All ways, all weathers blighted,
And only in them, the unhoused,
As earth and sky break,
That love at last, burning.

X

Drizzly Candlemas: and at once
Soil, giving off
A live smell, stirs.
Quick as birdthroat, to sing
At the sign, shoot and bud
Swell towards hidden light.

Close to the sea's edge even,
Grey, grey, grey,
A skylark flings at the clouds
Its fluttered scale, amid
Gulls' cackle, seasonless,
Then, more watery, fainter,
Wind-blown piping from waders.

Little signs, till the ivy,
Mat all winter, glistens
On boughs dark still, bare;
Till eyes prepare to look
Once more, and the sun connives.

Landscape? Now and then, changing.
System? Never, but here and there
A landmark — castle or nuclear station —
Of power, changeable too, of tillage,
Drainage, plantation, felling and demolition.

Real, the five bars of the gate
Standing yet between broken hedges
Though it bars nothing, nothing supports it,
Even the posts gone; and real,
For a while, its absence, the changed view
When the good woodwork's undone, burnt.

Real, the weathers, more than the season,
As long as they're left to turn between
Blighted earth, blighted air,
Blighted water, oh, and the fire
That blasts all, leaving no ashes
But blight again that will feed no growth.

And forewarned of blindness, theirs
Less than a gouged orb's,
Almost eyes refuse
The effort of looking.

Almost minds, forewarned
Of the void minds have planned,
Shrink from their work of naming —
Names for the obsolescent? —
Find it wiser to match
One void with another
And shelter within it, waiting.

Almost, forewarned less
Of their failure to hold
Than the shaped matter's, hands
Refuse their labour of shaping,
Twitch, jerk in a circle,
Fidget, botch, or fold.

Out of two jagged flights
A wheel of lapwings forms
In the grey sky and rolls
Eastward, from ploughed fields,
Wet pastures, to feed
And breed on the wilder marshes.

'Migration', a man notes,
'Transition', but in his heart,
As ever, protests that all
Must remain as it was, for ever,
Unless it increase, unless
The crested bird, iridescent,
Is joined, not replaced, by the brighter
Green, the yellow and red
Of the shy woodpecker,
Rarely seen on the ground;

And thinks of a death: hers
Who long resisted the flux,
Too, in her blood, her flesh,
And had gathered agate, amber,
Cornelian from shingle on beaches
To store at home, admire;
Yet, assenting at last, recalled
Not them, but the sea, the sea

That had room for more, for a city, once,
Abbeys, churches, harbour and market;
That swallows and breaks down, reassembles
And spews up again on some shore
Its refuse and progeny, dead or alive,
Could engulf an island, a continent
With all its creatures, true or mutated,
All its machines of industry, war,
Settle the mixture and nourish a nucleus.

But meanwhile sunshine has drawn
From land, from moist leafmould
An odour all darkness, earthy,
Of germination, mingled
With airy fragrance of snowdrop,
Wych-hazel, primrose
Even, when out on the moor
Still it is gorse that flowers,
Wintering; though cold winds
Will return before long,
Before spring, driven higher,
Brings a commotion of leaves.

Meanwhile midges dance,
Never counting the wingbeats,
Unconcerned with duration.
A weather they celebrate,
Their own nature, what moves,
Halts them, now and here,
What makes them one with the weather.

IX

Dream Poems

1961-1982

The Road

It begins near Venice,
A Venice of chasms and pools,
And above a coastline longer than vision
Gently curves
Into a south or east without end.
Always the question is
How far can I walk it
Across what frontiers
Into what vastnesses,
More golden mist,
Woods even denser, darker,
Mountains more mountainous
Above a more dazzling sea.

Always I am detained;
As by this new nation
Of displaced persons
Who are rarely visited,
Whose nationhood is a cause.
They needed me,
Appealed to my friendship,
Involved me in schemes,
Charged me with missions
To friends whom I never reached.

If only I could move on
To the wilder, more alien countries
Farther along the road.

Scenario

1

He came home. Came home? The house
Did not fit the garden, the view.
Their own, locked up in his absence?
Another she'd bought and unlocked?
On the floor of a half-lit room
Lay family silver, baskets full,
Tapestries, paintings he could not remember possessing,
A screen of beaten brass,
Concertina of Indian dancers,
Flimsy, garish, in half-relief,
All dumped there to be discarded
Or, if he chose, kept to furnish the house.

2

Threading his way to the garden through crowds of guests
He looked for his landmarks and frontiers:
To the north a great railway station
Linked to the house by a concrete road
That brought more guests in taxis.
To the south a valley and, hazily shining,
Cupolas, palace roofs, towers
Framed in mountain-tops, wooded ravines.

A woman stood near him, a stranger.
"Lend me your eyes," he begged her, "I mean,
Tell me, describe what *you* see.
My left eye fear, my right eye desire
Will not focus; all shifts and blurs.
Where am I?" She laughed, and moved on.

3

Room after room. Bare galleries, halls,
Passages, thronged with guests.

Unrecognized he explored them,
Came to an improvised kitchen
And found his wife with a man.
"Hallo," she said, and smoothed her lover's hair.

He turned on his heel, strode through the staring crowds
And, alone in the garden, waited.
They followed: a burly man,
A fence between them. He vaulted,
The man seized his leg, pulled him down,
Hurled a knife, then a pitchfork,
But felled by his fists, lay still.

The single boom of a gong.

4

Longer than sight the table stretched,
Between bare walls without end,
Faces, faces, to each of which now with an effort
He could have attached a name, a function, a place.
"So the three of you will be living together"
Neighed the sleek-haired one with a bow tie.
"It's hard enough to live with one's wife,
Let alone her lover" he heard himself answer.
A *bon mot*, apparently. Between their guffaws
He corrected himself: "But no reflection
On *my* wife. A general observation."
Had she heard him? He did not know where she was.

5

He walked with her and their only child, a daughter,
No house in sight, no intruder,
The three of them anywhere, walking in silence.
He turned to her: "Is it true ...?"
Needing her confirmation of the silence
That made her true again, gathered into a moment

Their moments and years.
"Quiet" she said, "not now — the child."
And knifeblade, pitchfork went home,
Pierced him with love, the first and the last pain.

The Search

As commanded, I looked for my origin,
Passed through the town in which my grandfather settled
And found no street that I knew;
On through the suburbs, blind bungalows,
Lilac, laburnum, narrowly flowering
And out into mountains, woods,
Far provinces, infinities of green.
Walked, walked, by day, by night,
Always sure of the route
Though the people grew foreign, bizarre;
And the birds, a species unheard of, remembered me.
At last I came to a village
Where they told me: here you were born.
An unlikely place — no petrol pump, office block, poster? —
Yet I could not deny it, and asked them the name.
Why, Mors, need we tell you, m o r s, MORS.

For No One

So we meet again, little girl
Whose blue eyes taught me
How to say nothing, to look
And be merged in looking.
I saw you there and I listened,
But you cannot hear me,
Nor do I know where you are.
No need, in that place
Where to look is enough,
Where to meet is a marriage
Nowhere, for ever,
Nothing can be undone.

Here, I should have passed by, unrecognizing,
You a woman now, still young but not beautiful,
With a bad complexion. But Beatrice was your name,
Recalled to me without words though your eyes were not even
    blue
And now you chattered gaily about yourself,
About living from hand to mouth, luxuriously.
Because you were Beatrice, nothing had changed between us;
Because nothing had changed between us, I knew your name.

Memory

My wives do not write.
Sweetly young, hair flowing,
They walk where they belong,
Riverside, lakeside,
Mountainside, hillside,
Woodland or grassy plain.

One I consoled —
Black-haired, sad
In her forest clearing —
Another I followed
From a wellspring up in the scree
To a pool's golden rushes.

Did I leave them, forsake them?
I travelled,
Remember no parting.
Ways, I recall, transitions,
The shadows, the colours turning,
Herbs acrid or heady,
Sweet wives the world over,
Sweet virgins walking where they belong —

Unchanged, unchanging regions,
And they unchanged.

But by the knee a stranger
Clawed me, held on;
I fought: my grappling hand
Slid deep into rotten flesh,
A hole behind his ear.
I knocked him down and ran,
Clegs covering me,
A grey crust;
Ran to the church, thinking
They could not enter there,
But still they clung, stinging,
And up I climbed, climbed
To the belfry, pursued
By a man half-decayed.

Sweet wives, sweet virgins
Walk still unchanged,
Do not write, do not miss me,
Never forget.
It was the sunshine, the shadows,
It was the herbs and the haze.

The Other Day

"I fell asleep in a flowering meadow:
Steely light, high up, was honing the swallows' wings.

I woke when dry twigs rattled,
Scratching the brickwork, a street lamp yellowed the wall.

Where have I been? Where am I? Flung like a stone
Through the days and weeks, late summer and autumn."

"You were ill," she said, "and now you are better.
Your weathers, your streams and your hills, they're all in your
    head.

On a welded frame you were born. Under a ceiling of plaster.
No bird flew there. Not even a bluebottle buzzed

On the clean glass. No bud broke from table or chair.
Heat was turned on, turned off. Like the light, the water.

Your children, look, have grown strong in their human
   seasons,
Content but for you. Waiting for you to come back."

"Back. Yank me back, then, through thunder and blizzards.
Blundering, wandering, blind in the rain, in the sun.

Black I was. Blacked out. Looking for blackberries, nuts,
In rooms painted white. And losing the flowers in my head.

The crazy daisies. The comatose roses. The funny
   honeysuckle.
Made in Noland for no one. No sooner seen than gone.

Give me time. Convince me that your time is mine.
Make me tick as the clock ticks — till the clock runs down.

Hold me, hold me, I'm falling. The swallows freeze in mid-air.
They've ploughed my meadow. The trees are bare."

The Blight

   Somewhere behind us, from the long room,
   Sear-frost, look! cried a child's voice
   As fingertips touching we stood
   At the window and looked,
   Felt the sap run again
   From the root up,
   New boughs burgeon under the new sun.

Sere-frost, in April?
There it was, icy rain,
And the leaves turned black, curled,
Bud, blossom shrivelled, fell,
Not one year's growth but the whole tree withered.

Your hand froze in mine,
Froze mine, yet tightened, the nails
Dug in through flesh drained numb,
Dug down to the bones and a deep nerve.

Let go, if you can.

Too slowly toward the root
Our death creeps.

Theogony

One feather, scarlet, on snow:
High rose the bird
That feeds by winter moonlight,
Warbles on farthest mountain tops,
By no man snared, by no man plucked or eaten.

One golden hair
Found on the pillow:
The woman gone, Diana of all that was hers
Grazes with absence the tiled floor
And hallows it, touched by her feet once.

By the Sea

For weeks now
In coves, in the deeper dips
Of the dunes, in cave mouths,
Daily almost, a corpse has been found,
Of a man, young or aging,
Of a boy. Mangled.
The cause of death?
Drowned, says one report,
Another, strangled.
Never afloat. Never bloated.

Called upon to investigate,
I combed the coast, came
To this rocky beach, saw
A line of bodies laid out,
Five, a green film
Covering each. Halted there,
On the low cliff, gaped,
Unable to move.
But one of them
Moved.
Slithered on to the next
And dug in, with nails,
Lips, teeth, gulping.

I yelled, yelled for a rifle to kill
The carnivore. Who sleek
As a seal, but
Girl-waisted now, girl
Breasts, girl buttocks
Outlined under the green
Slime, wriggled
Quickly toward the water,
Rippled away, merged.

Dream Houses I

They have a history, dream history
Of how acquired, when occupied
And why vacated, those haunted half-ruins
Inherited only from earlier dreams,
Half-obscured by a wilderness
That once was garden or park.

The precise location, boundaries
Are dubious, as are my rights
Of freehold, leasehold, mere lodging.
For strangers have moved in,
Families, communes, beside
Those nearest to me
Now or at any time,
She who left me, she whom I left,
He whose handwriting changed, he whom frustration bent,
Each with a choice between many faces,
Youthful or aging, never estranged;
And the dead cohabit there with the living.

Yet the great hall, higher than warehouse, chapel,
Hidden behind the façade, reached
By going down — a staircase wide, bright,
Not winding — remains inaccessible,
Because unknown, to the newer tenants.
That hall, the alluring extension
Of one house alone, is the heart of them all.
Its bare walls, floor of grey stone
Untouched by furniture, offer
Pure luxury, space
Enclosed, held, not by me,
To immure a silence,

home.

An emptiness?

There they are,
Invisible, the living, the dead,
In a house inhabited once
And mislaid like a letter giving
Details, dates, movements
That could consummate love.

Every meeting is there,
Every parting, the word
Hardly whispered, more sensed
Than heard: all retained by the bare walls
Of the hidden hall in the tall house
Mine and not mine.

Outside,
Where trees tower, meadows and heathland merge
In the foothills of high ranges,
The laughter of children hovers,
This muffled hammerbeat
Is their murdered great-grandmother, walking.

Dream Houses II

1

Deep down, underneath a cellar
Lay the remains of a corpse
Hidden there — with whose help? —
After a killing I had not willed
Yet had done — or never done? —
That had happened, in horror,
Revulsion, remorse at the doing,
Fear less of punishment
Than of the thing done, the knowledge
That unwilled it was done
By hands mine and not mine —
So long ago, I could nearly doubt it.

2

Into the house now — which house? —
My father, the doctor, has moved
From his death; and, let into the secret
By no doer, no helper, no spy,
Without one word, applies himself
To the deed's undoing, the resurrection
Of a bundle of stinking bones.
On to a bed he's carried it; and sits
On the edge, bends over it
Till by attention, care, he's infused
A breath that forms flesh.

3

So that was the victim — I had forgotten.
She's risen, she walks, an elderly lady,
Benign, and remembers no murder,
A guest in the house. She could leave.
Let her stay. For the staying proves
That our house is healthy now, healed
(That I am healed of the horror,
The deed done, never done).

4

Then the house cracked. (It was one left
Long ago, in the war, and demolished.)
As I washed my hands I heard
Bricks fall, and felt,
Deep down, a swaying, a sliding
Of beams. But trusted them still.
The floor I stood on held,
Water still flowed from the tap.

5

My life's houses are one,
The lived in, the left, the levelled.
In a lost garden, though,
Roses are flowering, in winter,
The leafage is lush.
In another I look for my children
And all my children are gone.
Ploughed fields, brown marshes
Up to the long horizon;
A lapwing flying.
Not a sound from the house.
Not a sound in the air.

Dropped In

This time it wasn't burglars
Who had forced the door
When I returned after midnight
To my room on the half-landing.

I saw light, heard voices —
Low, uncommonly low
If one of them was
Irving's, my friend's,
As I thought, the other
His latest girl's.

Ah, well. I knocked before entering,
But needn't have done.
Not to borrow, this time,
Not for so much as a meal,
Not for small-talk either
They had dropped in.
No, they had brought me something —
A corpse.

A young woman's, he said.
Killed, yes, but not murdered,
Killed in a game they had played.

I did not look, did not ask
Who she was, but knew
That I knew her, knew
That the body was under my bed.

Dumped there, for me, why,
If she died in a game?

Quick, call the police.
The longer you wait
The less they'll believe you.

The longer we argued
The more she was there,
The more she was mine
To be hidden or moved
And hidden again, to be touched
And, worst, to be recognized.

Take care, he said, going.
Of yourself — and her, said the girl.
One day you'll understand.

Nightmares

Private, at least they were truthful
In their way, the hitting of nails
Straight on the head, into
The live pulp of loves and fears.
Pierced there, "I" guessed how little "I" knew
What under the skin "I" was,
At best learned what to do
About the cells that regardless
Of "me" made their patterns, unmade them,
Played at growth and decay.

388

"I"'m not in them now. Not "me"
But the city they visit, aim
At its fabric of cells.

Two vehicles, bee-shaped, whizz
Through the air. One crashes
Into a tank on a rooftop,
Spews fire, drops to the ground,
Takes off again at full speed.
The other has flown on
To collide with an office building
Out of sight, out of earshot.

The streets are silent. The houses are silent.
The city they pound is empty.
Out of range, beyond
Human sense, human senses
Machines and concrete clash.

A metallic swarm has swooped
Down at the hive, to break it.

Night...

Night. A man clears a border, throwing
Plucked weeds, broken-off twigs of shrubs
Forward, against the wall of his house, against
That in the air which whispers: so late, so late.
Delinquent hands. Delinquency of hands
Driven to impose an order still on rankness
When, our own order lost, we are less than grass.
Labours in drum-taut stillness, pauses, and hears
Mated shrieks of barnowl and moorhen,
Vixen and leveret in the one dark's grip;
Knowing: lostness it is that keeps me, that holds me here.
Till another cry rips him, his own name

Called out again and again, in the house,
By her his absence has woken, who looks for him now,
Whom, so near, so near, he can summon no voice to answer,
No motion to comfort, his feet leaden with loss.

In No Time

A drifting it was, as though back into youth
But more free and easy, this terminal party
Thrown by no visible host, with couples
Forming and breaking up in no time
(In no time the party took place, at no place
Anyone there could have named or remembered.)
And he, adrift, almost at once had been drawn
To a dark-eyed woman with pale hair,
Talked with her, drifted off again towards others,
Seeing her deeply engaged with another man,
But she returned to him, closer to him than before,
And their talk flowed like one river's water,
Now eddying, rushing, now stalled in pools that look still
Over a bed so ancient, to them it seemed changeless.

Together they left, as one, their wishes, their thoughts
Wedded in no time (for time
Was about to end, to no end
They or anyone could have named,
No one will live to remember),
And by no audible word of command were drawn
Or driven into a garden —
His once, he told her — that was to be stripped, they knew,
Of all that grew there, species, hybrid or graft,
Down to the bare black soil, up to the branches,
Beyond their reach, of overshadowing trees.
(For light and the colours light played on for eyes
That colluded with light, with colours, would now be put out
And the eyes put out in no time.)

Worked, as one, towards the garden's unmaking,
Towards their own, so that bare as the black soil
They would be one indeed at the consummation,
Wholly in body and mind would share
Their every possession, none.

And the weather sickened, disowning the season,
Swallows hurtled and crashed as the air-streams collided,
The trees, together, shook off all their blight of leaves
On to them who, melting, dissolved in each other,
Were blind in no time, at one with their world.

Dying

So that's what it's like: hearing them talk still
In a whisper, and letting your love pick up
Crumbs in response from the bare table
Till — there are crumbs left, things to be said
And their voices are audible still and their faces
Clearer than ever — another need
Orders withdrawal, silence.
A bad joke, you think, this pretending not to be there —
And are gone, where they will follow.
Going, have punctured the bubble, time,
So that your wide-open eyes insist:
Speak louder, my near ones, laugh, and rejoice.